D0185582

The Art and Craft of

PAPER

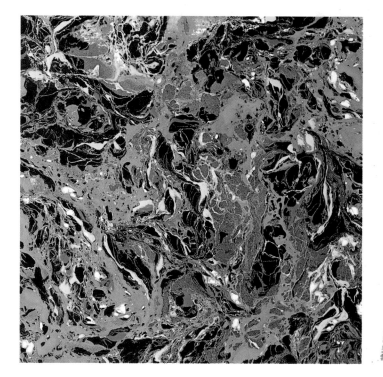

Block Printing
Pulp.
Photography
Techniques
Paper back
Hard back.

Paper
Materials
History of Paper
Origins
Decoration.
Decorating Paper.
Paper making
Marbling
Furniture
lampshades
boxes
Jewelry
Papier Mache
Books
Making bodes
book binding
Spraying

YEOVIL COLLEGE
LIBRARY

Yeovil College

Y0058200

The Art and Craft of
PAPER

Faith Shannon

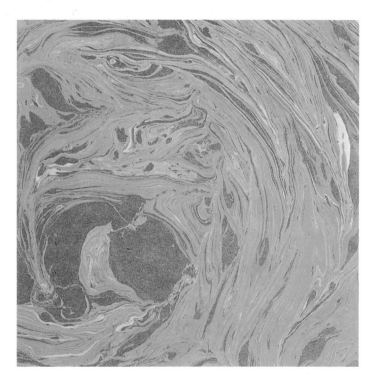

Photography by Peter Marshall

Mitchell Beazley
In association with Il Papiro

The Art and Craft of Paper
Faith Shannon
First published in Great Britain in 1987
by Mitchell Beazley
an imprint of Octopus Publishing Group Ltd
2-4 Heron Quays, London E14 4JB

Design Zoe Davenport
Executive Editor Robert Saxton
Assistant Editors Celia Van Oss, Frances Gertler, Anderley Moore
Production Philip Collyer
Illustration Kevin Hart

Papermaking and Marbling sections Jenni Grey
Copyright © Octopus Publishing Group Ltd 1987

Reprinted 1990, 1992, 1994
Reprinted in paperback 1996, 1998, 1999
First published as **Paper Pleasures**

No part of this work may be reproduced or utilized in any form or
by any means, electronic or mechanical, including photocopying,
recording, or by any other information storage and retrieval system,
without the prior written permission of the publishers.

A CIP record for this book is available from the British Library.
ISBN 1 84000 132 1

The publishers have made every effort to ensure that all the
instructions given in this book are accurate and safe, but they
cannot accept liability for any resulting injury, damage or loss to
either person or property whether direct or consequential and
howsoever arising. The author and publisher will be grateful for any
information which will assist them in keeping future editions up to date.

Typeset in Modern 216 by Dorchester Typesetting Group Ltd.,
Dorchester
Printed and bound in Hong Kong by Toppan Printing Co., Ltd.

CONTENTS

Y0058200

I can still remember the feeling and smell and even the sound of different papers from my childhood, when I used to while away hours making things out of paper to my own rules.

FOREWORD

It seems in retrospect that even as a child I was beginning to glimpse something of the infinite possibilities of paper. You can write on it, paint on it, draw on it, decorate it in an endless variety of ways, cover things with it, and make objects that are flat or three-dimensional. Paper – as I later came to understand – can even be used in building, and for making clothing. The Victorians made furniture out of it. In short, paper is wonderfully versatile – so much so that most of us tend to take it for granted. It repays a closer look.

My whole approach in this book stems from my experience of teaching bookbinding to students of diverse backgrounds. Those who are training in graphic design or illustration have an advantage in their willingness to experiment. But this is an attitude that anyone can develop, given the right encouragement. All my students have the same starting problems, but the less artistic ones tackle them in slightly different ways. Perhaps they are a little more inhibited, more anxious to "get it right". However, it isn't long before I can persuade them that even their mistakes can be useful – as reminders, or at best as starting points for something else that they may decide to make later on.

In *Paper Pleasures* I have tried to reflect the importance of learning by experience and experiment. I do not believe in offering a diet of didactic instruction worked out rigidly to the millimetre. Plenty of procedures and explanations are given in this book, but they are designed to clarify, rather than to straitjacket.

I'm also deeply committed to the importance of "feel". Paper almost *demands* close attention as you work with it. To exploit its full potential, you have to become engrossed, appreciating the distinctive character of the sheet you are working on by direct contact through the fingers. This is what I learned as a child. As a teacher, if I tell my students that a particular paper is expensive or precious, it's interesting to see how they change their attitude, handling the sheet with curiosity and responsiveness.

Whether you buy your paper from a supplier or try making your own at home, this is the kind of tactile awareness that paper deserves. As you begin to experiment with some of the projects suggested in this book, you will soon come to appreciate paper's astonishing versatility. And as your understanding grows, so will your enjoyment.

Author's acknowledgments

Many of the projects in this book have been made by mature part-time and first year Graphic Design students at Brighton Polytechnic, Sussex. I am indebted to them not only for their workmanship but also for their exciting ideas. These and other students have helped to give the book its shape. In particular, my thanks go to Harriet Topping, Gill Parris, Sue Doggett, David Lewis, Georgina Lee. Others, whose work could not be included, are to be thanked for taking part with me in the fun and experience of working with paper.

I am particularly grateful to Jenni Grey, an ex-student of mine and now a successful bookbinder with a growing reputation. As a mature student starting from scratch, Jenni showed a feeling for paper, a quality of craftsmanship and a sensitivity that her substantial contribution to this book amply reflects. She rose to all the challenges, assisted by her family, who inevitably got involved on the way!

Similarly, my own family, of necessity, have been surrounded by paper activities for months, coming home to saucepans of boiled paper instead of supper. My daughter Hannah Tofts created many of the pieces in this book. When a small child and now as a post-graduate MA student in Graphic Design, she responded to these projects with typical spontaneity, enthusiasm and imagination.

Another thank-you goes to Simon Green, who despite an extremely busy life has been kind enough to check the historical facts in my introduction. His integrity as a papermaker is respected internationally by many craftsmen and artists.

Last, but by no means least, my appreciation goes to the Mitchell Beazley team who showed such remarkable patience and concern in their work on the book.

Faith Shannon

PAPER IN PERSPECTIVE

A civilized world is inconceivable without paper. The uses of paper as a medium for storing and conveying information go far beyond the dreams of its inventors. And then, of course, there is the artistic aspect – paper as a means of self-expression, from notebooks and diaries to drawings, watercolours and other forms of fine art. Not to mention the exciting decorative uses – from lampshades to bowls, even picture frames – that are the subject of this book. Even in an increasingly computerized society, paper continues to hold its place of crucial importance.

A brief look at the long history of paper will give some idea of its unique and lasting place in our cultural development. The account that follows can do no more than sketch in the main outline. For a more complete picture, it is fascinating to turn, for example, to Dard Hunter's classic history of 1943, *Papermaking: The History and Technique of an Ancient Craft,* to which any survey must be indebted.

Paper and its precursors

Today, it is all too easy to take paper for granted. To communicate in "writing", we no longer have to carve laboriously into stone or wood, or make cumbersome tablets of clay or waxed wood in which to incise our messages, as earlier civilizations had to do. As the craft of papermaking took over from these methods, communication took a leap forward. Knowledge began to spread throughout the world. Paper not only made the written word more readily accessible, but provided the foundation for a later invention – that of printing. Eventually, the bookbinder adapted his ancient craft to printing, learning ways to work with paper in three dimensions to complement the printer's concern with surface qualities.

Until the printing revolution, an instrument such as a stick, a length of bamboo, a quill pen or a brush dipped in pigment was appropriate for writing. It was used with a surface, or "substrate", which one might mistake for paper, but only at a superficial glance. The precursors of paper, related only in that they also come from natural substances and provide a surface for writing or drawing, are of great interest. By looking more closely at them, we can better appreciate the nature of paper itself.

The best-known cousin of paper is papyrus, made from a grass-like plant – a versatile sedge, *Cyperus papyrus*, from which our word "paper" is derived. We tend to think of papyrus as coming from ancient Egypt, but the plant is also found elsewhere: the ancient Greeks and Romans used it too. The process by which papyrus was made to yield sheets for writing was different from the principles of papermaking.

In Egypt, where wood was scarce, papyrus was used in many ways. For example, it was burned as fuel. Even the root was valuable, being made into all kinds of utensils. However, the part that concerns us here is the stalk, which is tall, fairly thick and made up of several layers. These layers were carefully split, and flattened with muddy water from the Nile, which also acted as a gluing agent, holding them together. Each layer of the sheet of "paper" comprised strips of papyrus laid at right angles to the previous layer. The layers were built up in this way until the required thickness was reached. The whole was firmly pressed and allowed to dry in the sun. After dressing with a flour paste, the mat of papyrus was beaten flat and smoothed.

In other parts of the world, notably the Pacific islands and those parts of central America peopled by the Mayans, bark from certain trees was used to produce a writing surface (in the Pacific islands the bark was made into clothing). The processing techniques differed, although the principle was broadly similar. The inner fibres of the bark were beaten until they were paper-thin. This work was performed by women. The ancient Mayan paper made by this method was employed for books as early as the 1st and 2nd centuries A.D. A cruder version of the same technique has been continued in Mexico and Colombia into the 20th century. In the Pacific region, fine bark paper, as well as cloth or *tapa*, are made by beating the bark over specially shaped logs. Pieces were sewn together and decorated beautifully with natural pigments. Like most early "papers", these products were treated with care and used for sacred or special purposes.

Paper itself was eventually to supersede these early equivalents derived from papyrus or bark. However, there is one such historic substance that is still made – the so-called "rice paper" used for watercolour painting in the Far East. In fact, this is not made from rice but from the pith of a tree, *Fatsia papyrifera* finely pared in a spiral from the outside to the inside to give a length of thin "paper". This is then dampened and dried flat, then cut to size. In its damp state it is tough enough to be modelled into flower shapes; and because of its slightly absorbent qualities it is suitable for subtle tinting with watercolours.

In some parts of the world, animal skins rather than plant fibres have provided writing surfaces. They have been stretched on frames, de-haired, de-fatted and scraped, then dried. The most familiar of these animal surfaces is parchment, which requires additional treatment with lime. The hand preparation of parchment is immensely skilful work. It is still carried on today, but on a small scale. In the past, the wonderfully smooth surface of parchment has been used for exquisite handwritten and illuminated manuscripts. Scribes and illuminators still value parchment for quality work, despite its expense and its rapid absorption of moisture, leading to swelling and shrinking, and cockling of the surface. Akin to parchment is vellum, which is thicker and used for bookbinding more than for writing. Parchment is generally made from sheepskin, vellum from calfskin or goatskin.

All these cousins of paper are derived from natural materials that have been flattened, beaten or scraped. Paper, however, is created differently. Natural fibres are separated from their original growth pattern by soaking and beating, or macerating. They are then suspended in water to make a fibrous pulp; and by means of a sieve-like utensil, they are lifted out in an even layer from which the water drains away, leaving a matted sheet of fibres. This is allowed to dry. After further flattening it is ready for use. In essence, this is the craft of papermaking.

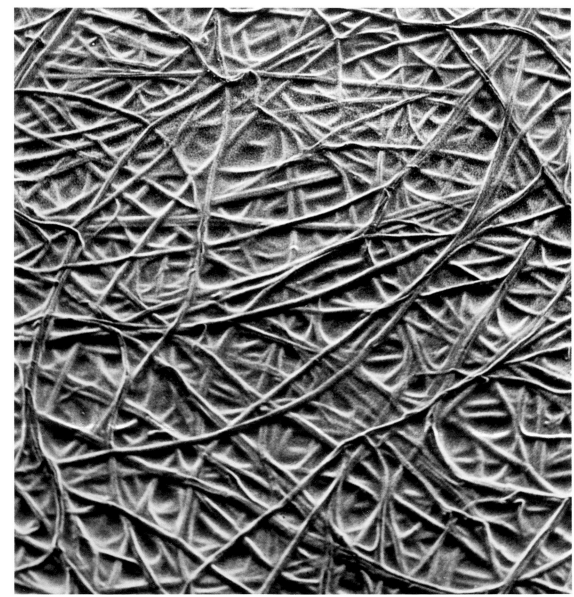

This magnified view of a sheet of paper shows the wood fibres from which most industrial paper is made. Plants, vegetables and linen or cotton rag more usually form the basis of handmade paper.

Origins

Paper came to the western world by a roundabout route from China, where it is said to have been invented in the 2nd century A.D. – although it is possible that its unrecorded beginnings go back much further. Before paper, the Chinese drew or painted their characters onto woven cloth, and it was perhaps the fibrous offcuts from the cloth that started everything in motion. Tree barks and other plant materials were also collected, as it was found that after maceration they could be made into thin, flexible yet strong sheets capable of giving a fine, smooth surface. In time it was discovered that images could be transferred to such papers by means of incised wood, ceramic or metal surfaces fashioned to receive and hold ink. It was thus that printing was born.

The finest early papers were treated with immense respect, and used to record ancient sacred texts. The more inferior grades were made into paper money, wrapping materials and clothing.

As knowledge of the invention spread from China westward along the trading routes, it filtered into other countries – Korea, Japan, Nepal, and thence to India in the 9th century. A century before that, papermaking had spread to the Arab world, and it was through Moorish influences via North Africa that it was belatedly to reach Europe. In the 12th century paper was being produced in Spain, and from there it penetrated France and Italy; then Germany and Switzerland; then Portugal and Holland; until in the late 15th century papermaking was first recorded in England. The age of the printed book on paper was heralded by the famous Gutenberg Bible in Germany in the mid-15th century.

In North America it was not until the European immigrants began to establish themselves that papermaking as we now know it began to develop, Pennsylvania becoming the first centre at the end of the 17th century. Other states soon took up the challenge.

As the craft spread over thousands of miles, the papermakers gradually refined their techniques, making constant modifications to equipment, especially to the main tool, the "mould", on which the mat of fibres was created. The oriental tools were adapted in various ways. Each century had its own innovators – too many to name here. An interesting development, in Italy at the end of the 13th century, was the invention of watermarks – the translucent designs we see on holding some papers up to the light. Watermarks indicated the maker and date, or the kind of mesh used on the mould in forming the paper, or were later used to counter forgery.

Mechanized systems of papermaking imitated the stages of hand production. However, machines brought about a distinct sacrifice of quality. To understand the crucial differences between handmade and machine-made papers, it is helpful to begin with some of the first principles discovered so long ago by the Chinese.

For papermaking to flourish, it must be based on a plentiful supply of suitably fibrous materials and clean, flowing water. Available supplies of a gelatine or starch size to reduce the paper's absorbency are also an advantage. The fibres mostly come from plants. Suitable materials include the fibrous inner bark of certain trees (such as some species of mulberry), the stems of plants such as linen, hemp or jute, and grasses – rye, wheat and so on – which produce straw. Leaf fibres such as esparto may also be used. Then there are seed hair fibres, the most useful of which come from the cotton plant. Also, there is wood – the basis of industrial paper production.

Of course, other materials of a fibrous nature are also suitable. The Chinese and Japanese have long used silk, which results in a fine and lustrous surface – and at the other extreme, some papers today are made of polyester fibres, which makes them tough and tear-resistant. There are also chemically produced plastic "papers", which are waterproof and exceptionally smooth for high-resolution printing.

The strongest papers are usually those with the longest fibres. Both the quality and the length of the fibres govern the final result. The early Chinese silk papers and the fine silk papers made today in Japan are flexible, light but surprisingly strong. For the most part, the earliest and strongest papers are those made from linen, cotton rag (recycled from woven cotton) and cotton linters (the shorter fibres not used in thread-spinning). These materials also form the basis of most handmade papers today.

East and West

The main difference in hand papermaking procedure between the East and West is the type of mould – the frame on which mesh is stretched. The structure of the mould affects the way in which a sheet of paper is formed and dried, and can govern the size of the sheet. The very earliest sieve or mould was probably a simple frame of four bamboo bars with a fine mesh of woven grass (*ramie*), secured at all four sides. The fibrous pulp made from the macerated plant was poured onto the mesh to make an evenly distributed sheet of matted fibres, which was then dried in the sun, and later peeled from the mesh.

The mould typical of China, Japan, Korea and India – and still found there today – is a frame of wood and/or bamboo crossed by a series of thin bars which strengthen the two longest sides and provide a support for a flexible cover. This cover looks rather like a rattan blind. Generally, it is made by laying thin strips of split bamboo rounded side up and lacing them together with horse-hair, silk, flax or other fine thread-like material. This is the "laid" mould, as we now know it,

The simple rectangular frames which form the mould and deckle are the papermaker's most important implements. The sheet is formed on the mould which has mesh stretched over it; while the deckle helps to shape the sheet.

as distinct from the woven version, known as the "wove".

The laid mould is dipped into a vat or container of pulp, then lifted out with a fine layer of fibres resting on the flexible slats. Excess water runs off the back of the mould. The layer of fibres can be removed by gently turning the mat, paper side down, onto a suitable drying surface. Then the mat is eased away from the fibres, leaving it free for further use. Sheets of paper made in this way are simply piled up on top of each other. After pressing, the sheets are separated out for drying.

The oriental type of mould can be more easily used for producing very long sheets, which are then cut as required. The paper used for Japanese windows and doors is made in this way to standard dimensions – long and narrow. Despite the incredibly fine, even character of the paper, the method of handling enables these long sheets to be made without damage.

The other type of mould is the rigid kind typical of Western practice. This comprises a frame of wood strengthened with non-ferrous (and therefore rust-proof) metal corner pieces and covered with stretched non-ferrous wires running the length of the frame. These wires are "stitched" together with finer wires and supported underneath by thin wooden bars, integral with the frame itself. A second frame without wires, called the "deckle", serves to restrain the pulp when lifted from the vat and to prevent it from running off the edges. It also determines the size of the sheet.

The "wove" mould came into use in Europe in the 18th century. It is capable of producing paper of a close-textured, even appearance, unlike the "laid" papers, which when held against the light reveal semi-translucent lines, caused by thinner deposits of pulp at the wires.

Rigid moulds require a special method of depositing the wet sheet of paper onto its

drying surface – which is generally a thick blanket called a "felt". Great skill is needed to transfer a sheet in one movement onto its drying base, leaving it there intact – the process known as "couching". The sheets are stacked in layers, interleaved with blanket felts, to a manageable height, and then pressed to expel water. After separating, and sometimes two further rounds of stacking and pressing, the sheets are cylinder-dried or dried between blotters. Then follow the finishing stages. Hot-pressing against shiny plates gives a smooth surface; or the paper may be left "rough" (felt-pressed) or "not" (cold-pressed to make it medium smooth). If the paper needs to be made less absorbent (as writing paper must) it will be passed through sizing tubs containing a thin, fine glue, or "size", made of animal hoof and horn or a synthetic substance.

There is a compelling fascination in watching a team of skilled papermakers in action, each with a specific task to perform. Anyone who spends time making paper will before long attain a level of success. However, it takes years of experience to match the expertise of the truly professional papermakers who practise the craft at its most refined level.

In its various forms, the mould is common to papermakers throughout the world. However, the methods of beating the plant fibres after they have been soaked and boiled to loosen unwanted particles, and to extract the cellulose, vary considerably. They include beating with mallets, grinding with stones, pounding with semi-mechanized beaters. Yet however primitive or sophisticated the means, the aim is the same: the fibres have to be softened and macerated so that they will form a fine matted layer. Skill is required in selecting suitable fibres, macerating to the correct degree, lifting up the right amount of pulp onto the mould and handling it properly afterwards.

Because of regional differences in raw materials and production techniques, handmade papers show a wide variation in character. The most obvious contrast is between Japanese papers, with their softness and distinctly fibrous appearance, and Western papers, which are harder to the touch and closer in texture. Japanese papers have to be more absorbent to suit a particular method of printing – they take woodcuts especially well. Western papers vary more in their surface finishes, offering a wide choice of textures, but lack the wealth of decorative finishes found in Japan. For writing, they are treated to a greater degree with size to prevent the inks from spreading – this is not necessary in regions where a brush is used for writing. Papers for hand printing of fine books are more absorbent than those used for writing.

The age of experiment
The dissemination of knowledge through printing, and rapid developments in printing technology, led to an increasing need for paper. Initially, cotton rag and linen supplied the demand, but before long other fibres had to be found. Some bizarre attempts were made from time to time to procure cotton and linen for recycling. In America in the mid-19th century, a New York scientist put forward the idea of recycling Egyptian mummy wrappings. Someone else following the same line of thought actually produced wrapping paper from mummies' linen bands and any papyrus manuscripts found with them!

It took several centuries of disparate experiments by a few dedicated men to show that many other plant fibres were suitable for papermaking. In 18th-century Europe, a Dr Schäffer produced books using paper from straw, cabbage stalks, asbestos – even wasps' nests. The wasp is believed to have suggested a route for further exploration into the use of wood pulp after some close

The photographs above show some of the stages in traditional Western papermaking.

Above left: *Pulp and water (known as "half-stuff") soak in a large beater called a Hollander. The automatic roller at one end speeds up the process of breaking down the pulp. The pulp is then transferred to a vat and the mould immersed in it (see page 34) to form the sheet.*

Above right: *Once the paper is sufficiently dry it is couched, or turned on to felt which soaks up the excess water. The coucher on the left is preparing the felt for the paper* on the mould in the background, which has been tilted prior to couching. The vatman on the right stands by with another mould. Up to ten sheets of paper a minute can be made by this method.*

Far left: *The paper is transferred from the mould onto the felt. Another piece of felt will be laid on top of this and a new sheet inverted onto it. Several sheets will be layered in this way.*

Near left: *When the pile of sheets has reached a manageable height, the last of the water is squeezed out by a hydraulic press.*

observations by a French naturalist of the 18th century, René Antoine Ferchault de Réaumur. He discovered that the wasp rasps wood to a fine state and binds it with a sticky secretion. On drying this material becomes, in essence, a fine paper. It was Réaumur who proposed that it should be possible to grind wood fine enough to produce cellulose for papermaking. Other important discoveries about fibres were made in London in the early 19th century by Matthias Koops, who experimented with straw from cereal crops, and whose research is considered to have brought about a breakthrough.

Alongside this hunger for new materials, there was the need to improve productivity. The first papermaking machine was a late 18th-century European invention. Nicholas-Louis Robert spent many years with St Léger Didot, a printer, developing various ideas with uneven success. Eventually, it was realized that Robert's dream was feasible. It would be possible to build a machine capable of producing a seamless length of paper on a continuous belt of mesh at a speed far greater than the pace of hand-producing single sheets. Robert's invention was taken further by some London stationers, the Fourdrinier brothers. Although some of the machines subsequently built carried the Fourdrinier name, the brothers gained no material reward for their important and lasting contribution to papermaking.

The papermaking machine soon became the basis of a thriving industry. The long-belt system was extended to one with a rotating mesh cylinder, with an internal drainage system which formed the paper as pulp came into contact with it. The layers of pulp were detached and passed on to a cylinder covered with felting, where a mechanized form of couching took place. The cylinder machine was initiated and refined in England in John Dickinson's mill in Hertford in 1806. It was secretly installed in America by Thomas Gilpin, who developed the English idea for use in his mill in Delaware in 1817.

Such machines opened up a range of new uses for paper – from newspapers and mass-produced books to paper collars and cuffs, boxes, even coffins and drainpipes.

Meanwhile, the search for raw materials continued. Many of the fibres from the "new" natural sources were usable only after thorough cleaning and bleaching to produce a white paper suitable for printing. Scientific methods of quality control became increasingly important. Printing and paper evolved in parallel.

Today, wood is the most suitable source of pulp. The longer, softer fibres are provided by softwoods such as spruce. Cotton and linen are still considered best for the finest papers, and some percentage of them is added to weaker fibres to increase strength. Straw, used before the development of wood pulp, still has a part to play owing to the competing demands on wood for the extraction of cellulose in the manufacture of synthetic fibres, cellophane, lacquers and varnishes.

Quality and quantity

That machine-made paper is indispensable there can be no doubt. If it were possible to use the finest fibres, it could be as long-lasting as any good handmade paper. The nearest the paper industry comes to this level of quality is in a machine-made imitation of handmade paper, called "mould-made". This contains good fibres, but tends to have the "grain direction" typical of machine-made papers – caused by the directional alignment of the fibres as the paper is formed on the travelling belt or the cylinder. Even though a machine simulates

This attractive fan-shaped paper and bamboo sculpture with its combination of different colours and textures, proves that there is no limit to the decorative and functional uses to which paper can be put.

the movement of a hand papermaker (as when the mould is skilfully shaken to distribute an even layer of pulp), the speed and directional pull of the machine tend to settle the fibres lengthways. Despite being matted, the paper will have a greater strength in one particular direction. And it will have less resistance to folding along the grain than across it.

The effect of water absorption is another point of difference between hand and machine papers. The cellulose fibres of paper are hollow and, when wetted, absorb water by capillary action. If the fibres are lying in a particular direction, as with machine paper, the expansion that occurs when the paper is dampened will be uneven – that is, it will swell more sideways than lengthways. There is thus a risk of distortion as the paper dries, and this must be carefully controlled if the paper is to be used for printing. With handmade paper, the distribution of fibres is even and therefore less troublesome. Then again, there is the question of resistance and flexibility: handmade papers generally handle much better than mass-produced ones, and are therefore more suitable for the finest books and paper artefacts.

The current volume of wood consumption for general-purpose papers poses increasing problems of supply. Tied in with this is the complex issue of the threat posed to the environment by vast plantations of softwoods grown for pulp. Research into other substrates for printing and packaging continues as a matter of some urgency. Recycling of paper is increasingly common, but much is still wasted.

Another cause for concern is the life expectancy of machine-made papers. Inferior papers, treated with chemicals that in the long run will be detrimental to the fibres, are unsuitable for the preservation of our culture. Today's standards of paper production are lamentable in contrast with those of earlier periods. The Gutenberg Bible, which has lasted since the 15th century, is a monument to the craftsmanship of an earlier age. This great disparity in paper quality was made abundantly evident by the terrible floods in Florence in 1966. Books and incunabula printed on handmade paper, centuries old, withstood the ravages of the floodwaters to a remarkable degree, only creating problems for the conservators when not aired and carefully dried immediately after the drenching. (In airless, humid conditions, mould grows very quickly in paper, causing the fibres to disintegrate.) The thousands of books made from machine-made papers and the coated shiny papers used today for printing were either destroyed or posed immense problems for the conservators.

It often takes a disaster such as this to alert people to problems and provide a catalyst for action. Thanks to the efforts of conservators working internationally to restore the magnificent historic books in the Biblioteca Nazionale di Firenze and other collections, our knowledge of paper and its constituents has been extended, and our interest in fine papers reawakened. Today we are still reaping the benefits of this resurgence in awareness. Artists all over the world are learning the techniques of papermaking and papercraft, and revelling in the versatility of paper as a medium for self-expression. Meanwhile, the ancient preoccupation with presenting ideas and knowledge in fine print continues steadily. Paper will always be cherished by the sizable minority who appreciate its beautiful visual and tactile qualities, and care about continuing a long tradition of excellence.

A close-up view of a pile of finished hand-made papers. Well-formed paper should be smooth in texture with a regular appearance. Its strength will depend on the fibres used to make it.

Understanding paper

To obtain maximum satisfaction from working with paper, you will need to familiarize yourself with the whole range of papers available, acquiring a feel for their different qualities and uses. Do not fall into the trap of thinking that machine-made papers are totally unsuitable for quality work. Good machine-made papers include a certain amount of cotton. In some of them, recycled high-quality waste paper forms the basis of the pulp.

In choosing paper for a particular project, there are a number of factors to consider, including grain direction, stiffness, translucency, texture, the size of sheet that will give you the most suitable working area, and the number of sheets you will need to buy. At this point, it has to be said that it is a false economy to buy really cheap paper: it is likely to be made from short-fibre wood pulp or poor-quality recycled pulps. Your local paper or art suppliers may be able to advise you on such matters. Before long, you will be able to recognize for yourself the papers to select and the ones to avoid.

Handmade paper comes in sheets of various dimensions based on historical precedent. There are some quaint names and odd sizes, which hopefully will not disappear into bland uniformity. The four sides are deckled. The colour varies with the pulp; sometimes there is added coloration, but usually the papers are subtle whites, creams, oatmeal buffs, quite often with a blue or green tinge. The thickness ranges from tissue-thin to almost cardboard toughness. Wide variations in texture and surface finish all help to make each sheet an enjoyable experience in itself.

The difference between "laid" and "wove" paper, to do with the type of mould or mesh used, has already been touched upon (pages 10–12). Essentially, "laid" paper, when held against the light, reveals a pattern of lines where the paper is thinner and hence more translucent. These are formed by fine copper wires (or thin lengths of split bamboo). Wove paper is more even in appearance, and might therefore be more suitable for some projects, especially those that reveal the paper's translucency.

If handmade papers prove to be too expensive for a project, there is another type of paper – known as "mould-made" – which combines the quality of handmade papers with the economy of scale that only mechanization can achieve. Mould-made paper does, however, have a grain direction. It is recognizable by its two parallel edges with uneven or "deckle" sides, in imitation of a handmade sheet. The other two edges are cut – reflecting a longer length of paper than is possible in handmaking. Despite being less expensive than handmade paper, mould-made paper is long-fibred and strong.

Whatever the paper you are using, you must handle it delicately. Try to develop that "finger lightness" that keeps paper looking fresh despite much handling. A well-conceived, well-executed project can be irredeemably spoiled by grubby fingermarks, "bruised" surfaces or dog-eared corners. It is preferable to pick up a large sheet of paper by diagonally opposite corners, allowing it to sag in the middle.

The grain direction of a sheet of machine-made paper is more than just a matter of academic interest: it will determine how the paper behaves when it is folded, torn or glued. In order to determine the grain direction of a sheet, place it on a flat, clean surface and loosely roll over one half, taking care to avoid creasing. With the flat of your hand, or with both hands, as though about to roll the paper into a tube, bounce-press it lightly. Try to remember what it feels like in terms of resistance to pressure. Let the sheet fall flat. Then turn it around 90° and repeat the process. With one of these two directions of folding, you will find that there is greater resistance or spring: this indicates that you are folding across rather than with the grain. To appreciate this, you may find it helps to visualize a sheet of corrugated cardboard – obviously, this would offer less resistance if you were to make a fold which is parallel with the tubes.

The grain direction will also become apparent if you fold the paper fairly sharply – but not too heavily – with your fingertips. Concentrate on the sensation of folding, as well as the appearance of the folded edge. Folding with the grain will produce an easy, smooth-edged fold that functions well and looks and feels right.

You can also identify the grain direction by tearing. Quickly tear a test area in two directions – along and across. You will see that one torn edge is smoother than the other: this is the edge that runs along the grain. Under a magnifying glass the nature and lie of the fibres will be quite apparent.

With just a few types of paper, it is more difficult to judge the grain direction, and you will have to resort to "dampening". You can use water, but if you do you will have to watch carefully, as the paper soon returns to its original state. You might find it preferable to use flour paste, which the fibres absorb more slowly, allowing you more time to observe the results. Tear or cut a squarish shape from the corner of the sheet, making a small mark at one edge and another mark on the corresponding edge of the parent sheet. Damp or paste one side of the test square and watch it curl. You will see that the curl will be *with* the grain.

Trying out these techniques for yourself on a variety of different papers is a useful exercise in itself. You will begin to understand something of the subtleties of paper – the inherent characteristics that accompany more obvious qualities of colour, texture and thickness. Only then will you be able fully to realize the creative potential presented by this perennial medium.

CONTINUING THE BEST OF TRADITION

Despite present-day technology, there will always be a place for traditional crafts-manship. The skills, materials and creative ideas of the past should never be allowed to fall into disuse, as the concepts of value, patience and quality they embody are eternal, and make an antidote to recent innovations based on cost-effectiveness.

The traditions of paper have survived in just this way. Small paper mills here and there continue the practice of making paper by hand following historic precedents. However, it is not only in the manufacture of paper that the best of the past remains alive, but also in its decoration. This is especially true of marbling – the ancient technique of decorating paper described in more detail on pages 82–93 of this book. Companies such as Il Papiro, the celebrated Italian marblers, pride themselves on their expertise in following ancient methods to reproduce authentic patterns of the past. The key to

success in such ventures is dedicated specialization. A veil of secrecy is also necessary, as it was in Renaissance times when rivalries in craft circles fostered espionage. Although the essence of marbling is universal – dropping paper onto a pattern of colours floated on a vat of "size" – there are many refinements and variations. Hence, secret ingredients play a part in the Il Papiro process, and these items of closely guarded knowledge are passed down from master to apprentice as in the golden age of marbling.

In its combination of traditional skills and modern marketing expertise, the marbling of Il Papiro demonstrates how the most cherished achievements of the past are robust enough to flourish even in today's highly commercialized environment.

Below left: Francesco Giannini (left) and Gianni Parenti (right) opened the first Il Papiro workshop in 1975 in the Via San Niccolò, Florence. The following year they started a more streamlined marbling operation in the Via Cavour. Since then, they have expanded their business with great success and have achieved inter-national renown for stationery, boxes and other objects covered with their own *marbled and other decorative papers.*

Below: In this view of the Il Papiro shop in Florence, a spectrum of vivid modern tissue papers used for wrapping, fanned across the time-worn surface of an antique wooden desk, makes a telling symbol of the old and the new harnessed together in the service of excellence.

Marbling depends on an unstable, liquid base of colour, which makes it difficult to produce a regular, repeated pattern that can be matched from one sheet to another. This sequence shows some of the basic stages followed in Il Papiro's Florence workshop. Only by long practice can success be obtained. The first step **(above left)** is to float the colours in the requisite pattern on a base of gelatinous size. This takes place in a special bath, to which a patterning comb is hinged. The preparation of the colours takes a great deal of experience: each decorator uses his own method. Temperature and humidity have to be rigorously controlled. The hinged, wide-hooked comb is drawn through the colours to take the basic pattern one stage further, creating swirled effects. By varying the comb size, different designs may be created. A finer comb, held by hand, is then drawn through the whole area of colours at right angles to the direction of the first comb **(above centre)**. A stick is used to further modify the design made by combing. It is at this stage that the characteristic "peacock's tails" of the Il Papiro style are formed. Next **(above right)** comes the laying of the paper, which has been treated with alum. This stage requires a steady, continuous, decisive movement, without interruption. The pattern of colours floating in the bath is transferred to the paper spread on top of them. White undecorated spots can form on the paper where air bubbles have been trapped between the two surfaces. To avoid this effect, any bubbles are pricked with a pin. After marbling is complete and any air bubbles removed, a metal rod is gently slipped under one edge of the paper and slid to the opposite edge. This helps to run off the small amount of size which would otherwise tend to adhere to the surface. With the aid of the rod, the paper is then carefully lifted, and hung up to dry.

PAPERMAKING

The art of papermaking has a long and interesting history, in the East, in Europe and in America. Nowadays, of course, most of our needs are met by papers made by industrial processes. However, handmade papers are still invaluable to artists and craftsmen. As you will yourself discover when working on some of the projects described in this book, the individuality of handmade papers can make them especially suited to particular techniques. If you look closely at a drawing or watercolour by one of the great masters, you will see how much use the artist has made of the rich texture of the paper itself.

There are limitations to the types and sizes of paper you can make as a beginner, but you will soon discover how satisfying making your own paper can be. Instead of being merely a surface upon which to draw or write, paper becomes something to be relished for its own qualities of subtle colour and texture – it may even become a means of expression in its own right.

The procedures given in the following section are simplified versions of traditional methods. Raw materials in papermaking include a wide range of plants, and fibres such as silk or even wool. Many such materials require extensive treatment to produce papers of acceptable quality, but in many cases this is a matter of patience and experience rather than specialized equipment. Cotton linters and recycled papers (avoiding poor-quality papers with a high wood pulp content) are easier to use for the absolute beginner. Some plant materials can be added for a more individual effect.

In essence, papermaking is simple. Once you have assembled the equipment (described on the following pages), all you need to do is prepare a pulp of clean material which has been mashed in a liquidizer so that the fibres are separated. You then lift the fibres from the water in a thin layer by means of a simple sieve in two parts – the "mould" and the "deckle". After draining, the layer of matted fibres is then dried, by one of several possible methods. It may be pressed if a smooth surface is required. To reduce the absorbency of the paper, which in its untreated form resembles blotting paper and would make ink or colour spread, a coating of starch or gelatine "size" may be added. These can be mixed with the pulp or applied in various ways to the finished sheet.

STARTING OFF

You will need:

Large tub, such as a washing-up bowl,
  leakproof and at least 6in (15cm) deep. A
  cold water storage tank of fibreglass is
  useful when making large sheets of paper
Liquidizer with a capacity of at least
  1¾ pints (1 litre)
Plastic buckets – at least two
Sponge
Mould and deckle (illustrated in next
  column). You can buy this item, or make
  your own as described on the opposite
  page
Sieve or colander
Curtain netting for lining the sieve or
  colander when straining very fine fibres
Whisk to agitate the pulp
Plastic bowls or glass jars, for storing
  excess pulp
Rolling pin

For pressing flat while drying, any of the
following:

Two wooden boards and heavy weights (e.g.
  house bricks)
Bookbinders' press (shown below). You can
  also make your own press, as described
  on the opposite page.

It is important never to use tools that might
rust. Even if no rust flakes drop into the
pulp, there is a danger that pollutants will
cause "foxing" (small brown spots) to appear
on the paper some time in the future. Paper
scientists are still unsure as to the exact
cause of foxing, but it is believed to be the
result of bacterial action within the sizing on
the cellulose fibres.

The mould and deckle

These are the only two items that you will
need to make at home or buy from a
papermaking specialist – all other pieces of
essential equipment are readily available.
The mould and deckle are simple rectangular frames of the same size. The mould has
mesh stretched over it; the deckle has no
mesh. Together they make a simple sieve:

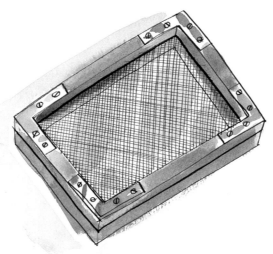

It is on the mould that the sheet is formed.
You can make paper on the mould alone,
without the deckle, but this makes the
process more difficult to control.

For first attempts, use the deckle, which
shapes the sheet, preventing the pulp from
running off the mould as it is pulled from
the tub. The distinctive irregular edge to
handmade paper (illustrated, top of next
column) is known as the "deckle" edge.

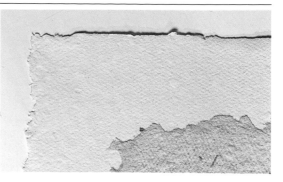

Before starting work, you must give some
thought to dimensions. The mould and
deckle must be small enough to fit inside
your tub, with some room for movement,
and a space of 5–6in (12–15cm) to the rim.
A frame of approximately 8 × 6in (20 ×
15cm) will fit comfortably into the average
large rectangular washing-up bowl. It is
sensible to begin with such frames – no
larger than A4 paper size – as they are easier
to control, and can be quite versatile. The
size of the paper when dry will be slightly
smaller than the inside measurement of the
deckle.

To make large single sheets, the mould
and deckle become difficult to handle on
your own without special equipment un-
suited to a small kitchen or workroom. You
can, however, join small sheets together
before drying, to form larger pieces: this
technique is explained on page 35.

You can make the frames of the mould and
deckle from strong picture frames or stretch-
ers. You must remove all traces of paint or
varnish from these so that there is no chance
that flakes will break off and spoil the sheets.
Strengthen any glued joints with rustproof
nails or screws. When you use old frames, it
does not matter if the deckle is slightly
smaller than the mould: but the deckle
should not be larger than the mould.

The best wood to use if you are making your own mould is mahogany, which is the most resistant to warpage and rot. Teak is also very good but any wood will do as long as it isn't knotted or twisted. For a small frame you can use wood of ⅜ × ⅜in (1 × 1cm) section, with the corners simply pinned together; ¾ × 1¼in (2 × 3cm) should be strong enough for larger frames that one person can hold comfortably. You will need to strengthen the joints with corner braces, or flat L-shaped braces.

experiment, but beginners are advised to start with a coarse screen which will yield a coarse-fibred paper. Finer screens will produce a more delicate surface, but you will find it more difficult to achieve a regular appearance.

On larger frames it may be necessary to support the underside of the mesh with thin strips of dowel, to prevent the mesh from sagging as shown below:

keep it as taut as possible. Secure one of the short sides of the frame first, then pin along the longer sides with brass nails or copper staples, before stapling down the fourth side.

Making a paper press
To produce a flat sheet of paper, you need to keep it pressed firmly while it dries. You can improvise a press using two sheets of formica – or two wooden boards with sheets of plastic to prevent them from getting wet. Any heavy objects can be used as weights.

Alternatively, you can make your own paper press. Two different types are shown below. In the first, four G clamps are used with wooden boards or plywood. Inside the press, paper and felt are alternated.

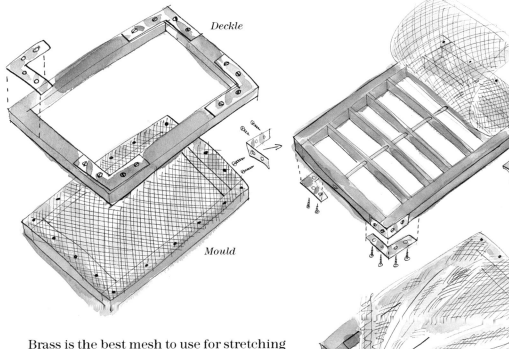

Deckle

Mould

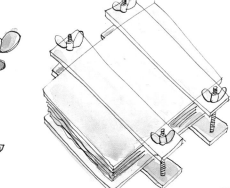

The second type of press uses strips of hardwood and wing nuts instead of G clamps. The hardwood strips prevent the boards from bowing at the centre.

Brass is the best mesh to use for stretching over the mould, but aluminium works well and is less expensive and easier to get (car accessory shops stock it for repair work on car bodies). There should be 30–65 per sq. in. (5–10 holes per sq. cm) Fabric mesh such as curtain netting, silkscreen mesh or plastic mesh are also suitable: look for 65–90 per sq. in (10–15 holes per sq. cm). Each of these meshes will create a distinctive surface on the paper. There is plenty of room for

If using curtain netting, wet it before stretching over the mould or it will stretch and sag in the wet pulp. While attaching the mesh,

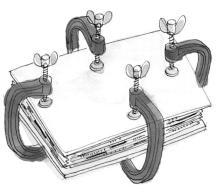

25

Recycled papers

This is a cheap and straightforward method. Almost any paper can be recycled. Computer paper is eminently suitable as it needs to be strong and therefore has long fibres; other suitable base materials are brown wrapping paper (unless it has a high wood fibre content), paper bags, carrier bags and envelopes. Avoid anything with a shiny surface, as it has probably been heavily coated with china clay, which may cause powdery patches on your finished sheets.

Paper that has been printed is also suitable but do not use anything that has been printed too heavily. Newspaper can be useful as bulk when combined with other materials. It can also be used on its own, but not when you require strength. Never use it to make paper of any lasting value, as its high acid content will cause it to break down within a short time. Newsprint will turn grey when pulped, and pink newspaper will take on a brownish colour when dry. You can remove the ink by boiling the pulp in a detergent solution: about 2 tablespoons for each 7 pints (4 litres) of water. A scum will rise to the surface consisting of a mixture of ink and detergent, and you will need to skim this off. Then wash the pulp carefully according to the instructions given for plant papers on page 28.

1 *Remove any residue of glue, staples, or anything else that may spoil the final product or damage your equipment.*

2 *Tear the paper into pieces approximately 1¼ in (3cm) square, and soak them in water overnight. Soaking for longer will further break down the paper, but don't leave it for longer than a week or it may begin to smell. The soaking period may be shortened if you pour boiling water over the paper and then leave it for a couple of hours, or you could boil the paper in a large rustproof saucepan for about half an hour.*

3 *Liquidize the soaked paper a little at a time. Start with around 10–15 pieces of paper for each 1⅓ pints (¾ litre). You will soon be able to judge how much paper can be comfortably liquidized in one batch.*

The machine should not be allowed to labour. If you are causing it to struggle, you may damage it and the paper will be broken down unevenly. Begin by liquidizing for 15 seconds. If there are still lumps of paper suspended in the pulp, liquidize for longer. The pulp should be of a smooth, creamy consistency. Although precise timing is not critical, you should avoid liquidizing for too long: the more you break down the pulp, the shorter the fibres become, and the weaker the paper.

Cotton linters

These ready-made sheets are well worth buying if you expect to make paper in quantity. To reduce the expense, you can mix them with recycled or plant pulp, and if you do this 2 pounds (1 kilo) should last a long time. Cotton linter fibres are much longer than those formed from recycled paper, and thus add strength to handmade paper. This quality makes them particularly valuable as an ingredient in delicate plant papers.

To turn cotton linters into pulp, simply take a piece about 6 in (15cm) square from a cotton linter sheet, tear it into pieces and liquidize in 1⅓ pints (¾ litre) of water. The pulp, having been left for a few minutes to absorb the water, is now ready for use.

Storing excess pulp

Pulp can be stored, but will smell if you leave it a long time. If it does smell, wash thoroughly before use. If very smelly, add a little bleach, leave for about an hour, then wash. To prevent pulp from rotting, add formalin (or formaldehyde) – just a few drops for every 2 pints (1 litre). Alternatively add one teaspoon of baking soda and one teaspoon of ascorbic acid.

You can save pulp in a much denser form than is needed, by straining through curtain netting. Refrigerate in a sealed container.

Dried pulp can be stored indefinitely. Strain it, squeeze out as much water as possible, and hang it up to dry. Before using, soak and reliquidize. The photograph below shows two pieces of pulp which have been dried in this way:

Even newspapers can be recycled to make fresh sheets of paper, whose appearance varies according to the precise composition of the pulp. This is a good way for beginners to try out the basic techniques of paper making. In this photograph, the right hand paper on the top row was made from a newspaper printed on white paper. Adding just a tiny quantity of plain black paper to the pulp produced a significantly darker effect (bottom right). A pink newspaper — such as the Financial Times — gives an attractive browny effect (top left). To make the central sheet shown here, scraps of paper were added to the pulp after liquidizing. All these examples were dried naturally, without weights.

PLANT PAPERS

You will need:
Large, unchipped enamel or aluminium
 saucepan
Scissors
Curtain netting
Colander or sieve
Mug or jug
Plastic or wooden spatula
Measuring spoon

For tougher plant material:
Caustic soda
Rubber gloves
Meat grinder (optional)

There are many plants that you can add to recycled paper or cotton linter pulp with little preparation. For example, flowers such as bluebells and cherry or apple blossom can be liquidized for a few seconds and added directly to the prepared pulp. You can also use the stalks, if they are soft, but first you will need to cut them into lengths of about 2 in (5cm). To form a highly decorative paper, save some of the flower heads and sprinkle them on top of the pulp before agitating it. Papers made from plants or flowers must be pressed and dried under weights (see drying method 3 page 37), just as dried flowers are. They can be delicate and brittle when dry, so it is inadvisable to use more than half as much plant as pulp mix.

You can either use plants straight after gathering or you can store them. If you plan to leave them for a short time only, cut them up into 2–4in (5–10cm) strips and leave them to soak in water. For longer storage, leave the cuttings in a pile outside. The plants will begin to rot and ferment after a while and the smell will be unpleasant, but this is a natural way to release the cellulose, and will shorten the preparation time. (It is, of course, advisable to wash rotting plants thoroughly before use.)

Preparing the plant material

Some plants such as celery, leeks and rhubarb, will break down fairly quickly when boiled and can produce quite varied results, as shown on page 31.

1 *Cut the stalks into 1–2in (2–5cm) lengths and boil them until they have broken down into strands.*

2 *To wash away the non-fibrous material, place some curtain netting inside a colander or sieve, pour in the boiled plant material, and rinse gently until the water is running clear.*

3 *Gather the corners of the net together to make a "bag", squeeze out the excess water and rinse again. Repeat until all the soft, surplus plant material is washed out.*

The remaining fibres will constitute only a fraction of the bulk of the plant material before boiling. You can mix them with the paper pulp as they are to create a decorative paper with a strong character, or you can liquidize them first to make a more delicately textured sheet. Again a 1:1 ratio of plant to paper pulp is a good starting point for experiment.

This collection of papers made from dried flowers suggests something of the range of plant papers you can make at home without difficulty. Sprinkling flower petals over the pulp before making the sheets adds to their decorative and original character.

PREPARING TOUGHER PLANT MATERIALS

Plants such as straw, cornstalks or ferns require more boiling to break down the usable fibres. Cut the material into 2—4in (5–10cm) strips. With really sturdy plants it may be advisable to mash them with a mallet.

It is best to boil the plants without chemicals in case they spoil the paper, but the process takes hours. You can speed things up by adding caustic soda to the pan before boiling, but be sure to wear rubber gloves and an apron when rinsing out the plant fibres: splashes on hands or clothes will burn. Do not exceed the quantities given on the packet. As a general rule, you should use no more than one tablespoon to 9 pints (5 litres) of water. It is better to err on the side of too little: you can always reboil the plant material, but *too much* caustic soda will damage the fibres irredeemably. Wash the plant fibres thoroughly after boiling to remove all traces of the chemical. If possible set the colander under a gently running tap for about 15 minutes, squeezing out the material at intervals throughout the rinsing, as described on page 28.

You can experiment with other ways of breaking down the fibres. Try grinding the pulp with a meat grinder, either before or after boiling. If you boil and *then* grind, it may be possible to make some coarse-textured sheets without liquidizing. Some materials, such as straw, can be used on their own, but it is advisable to add some finely liquidized paper pulp to fill in any small holes.

This paper is purely decorative, being too fragile to serve any functional purpose — it is simply a mat of plant fibres, from dead leaves that have been boiled and coarsely liquidized. The absence of any pulp has caused a loosely woven effect, with large open spaces.

The element of chance is part of the enjoyment of making paper from plant materials. It is a good idea to make concise notes about each type of paper you make, so that you can repeat a process when the results are satisfactory. However, even with notes, you will find it difficult to match different batches of pulp.

The plants used for the papers here were boiled until soggy, and some of them then liquidized, before being mixed with recycled paper pulp. The materials were:

1 *boiled leeks*
2 *onion skins, boiled and liquidized*
3 *leeks boiled and liquidized*
4 *autumn leaves, boiled and liquidized*
5 *boiled rhubarb*
6 *autumn leaves left to stand before being boiled and liquidized*

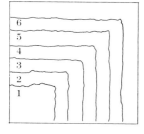

Tougher plant materials, such as straw, require special treatment to break them down into fibres usable for paper-making. The making of these three straw and three wild flower papers was speeded up by adding a small quantity of caustic soda before boiling, as described on page 30. In the case of the wild flower papers, the plant pulp was mixed with liquidized paper pulp.

1 wild flowers
2 wild flowers
3 straw
4 straw
5 wild flowers
6 straw

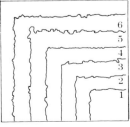

FORMING THE SHEETS

The liquidized pulp should be a suspension of fibres in water, blended to a creamy consistency. The thinner the pulp, the more delicate the sheet formed. To begin with, aim for the layer of pulp to be about ⅛in (2–3mm) thick on the mould. If the pulp is too thick, add more water to the vat. If too thin, drain off some of the water and add more pulp. Once the first batch of paper is dry, you will see how the thickness of the pulp layer relates to the paper thickness.

If you want all the sheets of paper to be the same, you must ensure that you liquidize enough pulp before you start, and mix it all together. You will need some extra buckets to hold it all. If you aren't worried about slight variations between the sheets, you can make the pulp as you go along, topping up the vat from the liquidizer as necessary.

If the sheet is badly formed, you can reuse the pulp. Just invert the mould onto the pulp in the vat: as you lift the mould away, the pulp will fall back into the vat and mix itself in. If you've already pressed the sheet, you cannot return it directly to the pulp like this: it will not remix evenly. Instead, liquidize the sheet for about 5 seconds beforehand. But remember that liquidizing breaks up the fibres, so the finished sheet will be weaker.

Get into the habit of washing the mould and deckle after each use, to prevent any transfer of pulp residue between batches.

Steps 1–8 cover how to make your sheet, whichever drying method you choose to use. (Drying is described on pages 36–37)

1 *Fill the vat with pulp so that the mould and deckle can be immersed easily, but not less than 7–8cm (3in) below the top of the vat, or it will splash all over the place when you pull out the mould and deckle.*

2 *Stir the pulp by hand, or agitate with a whisk. Work quickly before the pulp begins to settle to the bottom of the vat.*

3 *Place the deckle over the mould next to the mesh, hold them firmly together and immerse them vertically into the far side of the vat.*

4 *Keeping all your movements as smooth as possible, tilt the mould into a horizontal position, pulling the frame towards the front of the vat until it is thoroughly immersed, then upwards out of the pulp.*

6 *Keeping the mould horizontal, give it a quick shake from side to side and front to back, as shown above. Ensure that you do this before all the water has drained through and the pulp has begun to stiffen. This action, which is known as "throwing off the wave", evens out the pulp and disperses the fibres, preventing them from all lying in the same direction.*

7 *Hold the mould and deckle over the tub, slightly tilted, to allow excess water to drain away from the pulp.*

MAKING LARGE SHEETS WITH A SMALL FRAME

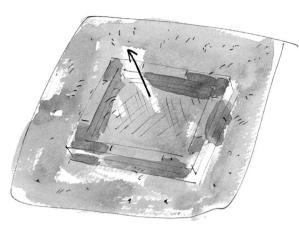

5 As you lift the mould out, the suction which helps to pull the fibres onto the mesh can be quite strong. The pulp will still be fairly runny.

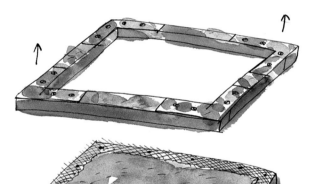

8 Put the mould down on a flat surface, and carefully remove the deckle from the mould, making sure that no drips fall onto the covering of pulp left on the mesh. If any drips do fall at this stage, they will displace fibres, causing holes to be formed in the paper.

To do this, you have to form the sheets without using the deckle. The edges will be very ragged and soft, and will thin out considerably.

1 Place a wet all-purpose cloth on a formica or perspex board. Check that you have enough room all round for your large sheet. If you do not wish to be limited by the size of the all-purpose cloth, dampened curtain netting, blankets or cotton sheets can be used instead.

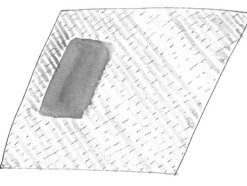

2 Transfer your first sheet close to the top left-hand corner of the cloth.

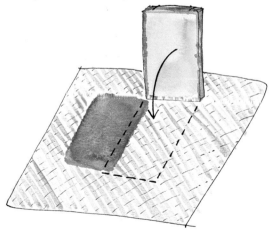

3 Form a second sheet on the mould, and place this next to the first one, allowing the edges to overlap slightly.

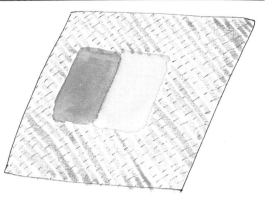

4 Continue building up the sheet in this way until you reach the required size.

5 It is better to press these sheets before drying, as this will strengthen the joins; however, this is not essential. Large sheets made on netting, blankets or sheets, can be dried on an indoor line, provided that you support the base cloth with pegs along the length of the sheet.

DRYING

The traditional drying method, known as couching, involves transferring the sheet from the mould to a humped blanket. Felt is then placed on top of the sheet, another newly made sheet of paper on top of that, then more felt, and so on. This sandwich is pressed beneath weights.

Couching was devised for paper-making on a large scale. For small-scale production there are easier, more convenient methods.

Method 1

You will need:
Extra moulds
Newspaper
Palette knife

1 *Leave the mould to stand on a pad of newspaper, pulp side up. The newspaper will soak up moisture from the mould, so you will need to replace it a few times before the sheet is dry.*

2 *When most of the excess water has drained from the mould and sheet of paper, it is safe to tilt them. Prop them against a wall or beside a cupboard to finish drying. However, take care that the pulp is fairly dry, or it will slip.*

3 *When the paper is completely dry, carefully slip a palette knife under one edge of the paper to loosen it from the frame, then gently ease the sheet of paper away from the mesh.*

Method 2

This method is suitable if you are making more than one sheet and you have only one mould and deckle.

You will need:
Indoor drying line
Clothes pegs
All-purpose disposable kitchen cloths – the less textured supermarket brands are the best
Formica or perspex board at least 2in (5cm) larger than the mould all around
Sponge

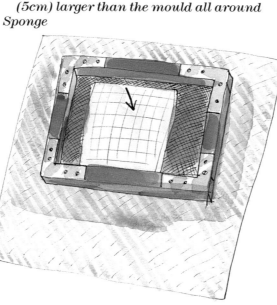

1 *Have a wet all-purpose kitchen cloth ready on your board. The cloth has to be wet so that when you place wet pulp on it, it won't stretch or shrink and pull the sheet out of shape. It also reduces the risk that the fibres will tear when you transfer the pulp from the mesh.*

2 *Invert the mould onto the cloth. Press a sponge carefully over the mesh, absorbing as much water as possible. This will form a vacuum between the formica (or perspex) board, the pulp and the mesh.*

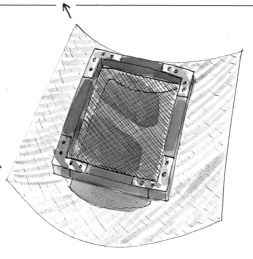

3 *Lift the corners of the cloth away from the board to release the vacuum. The mould will spring away from the pulp which will have adhered by suction to the cloth.*

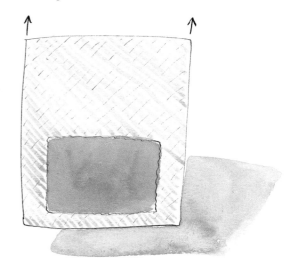

4 *Peg the cloth on an indoor line to dry. Use a tub or sheet of newspaper to catch the drips. When the sheet of paper is dry, place it face down on a flat, clean, dry surface and delicately pull the cloth away from the paper.*

Method 3

You will need:
All-purpose kitchen cloths
Formica or perspex board larger than the mould
Plenty of newspaper or blotting paper or (preferably) pieces of old blanket, at least 2in (5cm) larger than the mould all round
Pressing boards: plus weights. Teak is recommended but melamine- or formica-covered plywood boards are also good

1 *Place a whole newspaper and/or blanket to a thickness of ¼in (5mm) on top of one of the pressing boards. If you use both newspaper and blanket, put the blanket on the top so that it is nearest to the paper – newspaper cockles very easily when wet and may cause creasing or cockling in your sheet if it comes into direct contact with the newspaper for too long.*

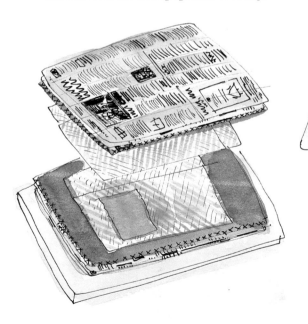

2 *Follow drying method 2 up to and including the transfer of the sheet to the wet kitchen cloth (step 3). Place the sheet and cloth*

on the newspaper or blanket, pulp side up, place another wet cloth on top of the sheet, then another layer of newspaper or blanket (or both) on top of that.

3 *If using blankets, continue layering until all the sheets are made and stacked; if using newspaper, stack just 3–4 sheets at a time. Place the second pressing board on top of the pile, and transfer to a press to squeeze out as much excess water as possible. If no press is available, stand on the pile for a couple of minutes; or pile heavy weights on top.*

You can now hang the papers out to dry, as in method 2, or spread them flat over newspapers or blankets. Or you can dry the sheets under weights, as follows; this takes longer, but the finished sheets will be smoother and flatter.

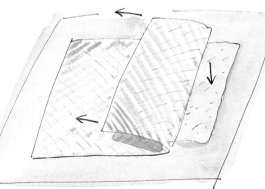

4 *Before placing the papers under the weights, let them dry for a few hours. While they are still quite damp, replace the cloths with clean ones of the same type, by placing each sheet face down on the new cloth and peeling away the wet one. You could use blotting paper instead, but this will make thin paper cockle.*

5 *Stack the sheets with their separating cloths between pressing boards as before. Put weights on the top. Do not leave them for too long in the press or under excessive weight lest they fail to dry out in the middle. If extra pressing boards are available, place them within the stack: this will further help to prevent cockling.*

6 *After a couple of days, you can remove the extra boards and separating sheets, and leave the nearly dry sheets of paper to finish drying between the two boards. Drying time will, of course, depend on the thickness of each sheet of paper and the number of sheets in the pile.*

Checking the paper quality

When the paper is dry, hold it up to a strong source of light. The thinner areas of the paper will be more translucent. If the sheet has lots of irregular patches, it is not well-formed. There are two common reasons for this:

a The pulp wasn't evenly suspended in the vat when the mould and deckle were immersed, or

b The "throwing off the wave" action wasn't adequate so that air bubbles were formed between the pulp and the mesh.

If the paper is thicker in one corner of the sheet than the others, it is likely that the mould wasn't horizontal when you pulled it from the vat.

If you find that your paper is always thicker in the middle of the sheet, the mesh on the mould isn't taut enough, and is sagging with the weight of the pulp.

Unless you have pressed the sheets of paper, they will have quite a rough surface. Even when pressed, the surface will not be as smooth as machine-made paper.

If you require a particularly smooth surface, you must first press the sheets as described in drying method 3 (page 37), then work each sheet of paper separately.

1 *Lay the sheet, still adhering to its all-purpose cloth, face down on a smooth surface, such as a formica board or perspex sheet.*

2 *To ensure that no bubbles of air have formed, press all over the sheet carefully by hand.*

3 *Firmly press the sheet down onto the board with a rolling pin, working from the centre outward to the edges, taking care to avoid creasing.*

4 *Carefully peel away the all-purpose cloth and leave the sheet of paper to dry on the board.*

5 *When drying is complete, peel the paper away from the board. The sheet should be as smooth as the surface on which it was pressed. Ensure that the paper is completely dry before attempting this last step, or you may crease or tear it.*

SIZING

This seals the surface of the paper, preventing water-based paints and inks from bleeding into it and creating feathery edges on every line you draw. There are a number of different substances that you can use for sizing paper. Easiest to obtain are ordinary gelatine, household starch, wallpaper cellulose adhesive, or PVA. These should be mixed according to the method described on the packet, but the quantities needed will vary according to the method of application and the type of pulp. Approximate quantities are given below but experience will help you judge better for yourself.

Sizing in the vat

Add dissolved size to the pulp so that the sheets are formed and sized in one operation. The following quantities assume that you are using a large washing-up bowl as your vat.

Gelatine: half a packet dissolved in a little hot water before it is added to the vat.

Household starch: mix one tablespoon in a little hot water.

PVA: Dilute one dessertspoonful before adding it to the vat.

While this might seem the easiest way to size paper, it does have its problems. If you are using gelatine size, you must use pulp that is still hot from boiling and work quickly, otherwise the size may begin to solidify, forming little lumps of jelly in the paper. Too much size can make the pulp sticky, so that it is difficult to remove from the mould. Sometimes the size does not disperse evenly through the pulp, although you will only notice this when you come to use the paper. Finally, if you add size to the pulp, it is

obvious that the whole batch will be sized; but for certain uses, such as printing, unsized paper is better.

Sizing after paper formation

This takes longer but has several advantages: sheets from a batch of pulp can be treated individually, sizing after papermaking adds strength to the sheet and usually seals the surface more evenly. Before you start, make sure that the paper has been left to dry for at least three weeks so that it is well settled. Otherwise it may disintegrate.

The various methods of sizing after paper formation are described below – painting, spraying and two methods of tub sizing. For each method, you can use any type of size: gelatine, starch or PVA.

Painting size onto the sheet

This is the easiest method of all, but time-consuming. Use a soft brush not a bristle brush, which may damage the surface of the paper. With this method you can apply the size more thickly and evenly than by spraying. It is particularly valuable on occasions when you are sizing paper for calligraphy, as some calligraphic inks do tend to bleed alarmingly.

Spraying size onto the sheet

You will need:
Plant spray or cheapest type of airbrush: do not use an airbrush you intend to use for delicate artwork
Formica board and plenty of waste absorbent paper (preferably unprinted)

The size must be fairly thin so that it does not clog up the nozzle of the spray. For a really fast method, use spray starch, which you can iron dry. You can also use a spray of fixative, but this contains substances that are likely to damage paper in the long term; avoid on papers for use in bookbinding.

Tub sizing

Mix the size according to the directions on the packet but water it down considerably: for example, one packet of gelatine might call for 3-5 pints (2-3 litres) of water. The dissolved size should not be too sticky. The basic idea is to pour the size into a shallow dish, such as a photographic tray, and dip the paper into the size. However, if you handle the sheets too much while they are damp, you could damage them. To avoid this, follow either of the methods described below.

Method 1

You will need:
Shallow dish
2 sheets of perspex. These must be smaller than your dish but larger than your sheets of paper
Wooden slats
All-purpose kitchen cloths
Newspaper

This is very messy so either work outside or have plenty of newspaper covering the floor or work surface. The "sandwich" of paper and perspex will be heavy, so don't attempt large batches by this method.

1 *Lay a sheet of perspex on the base of the photographic tray filled with the size. Resting the perspex on two wooden slats will make it easier to lift out again.*

2 *Carefully place the sheet of paper in the size and push it down onto the perspex.*

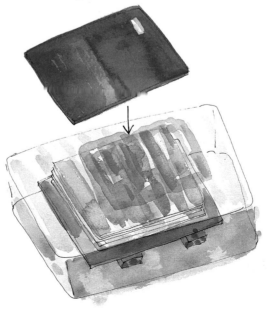

3 *Repeat the process, building up the pile of sheets until they have all been sized. Place a second sheet of perspex on top of the pile and lift out the whole lot together.*

4 *Press the pile for about ¼ hour, then remove the top sheet of perspex and carefully separate all the sheets. You can either leave them to dry separately on absorbent paper, or re-stack them and leave them to dry under weights as in drying method 3.*

Method 2

You will need:
Shallow dish
All-purpose kitchen cloths

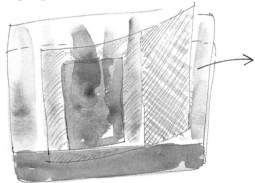

1 *Lay the sheet to be sized on an all-purpose kitchen cloth, then place this gently on the size with the paper uppermost. Remove after the size has soaked through into the paper.*

2 *This method tends to leave bubbles on the surface of the paper, so lay another all-purpose cloth on top of the sheet and press out the bubbles by hand, or with a rolling pin.*

POSSIBILITIES WITH PULP

There are various ways to manipulate the appearance of paper while you are making it. You can experiment with these techniques to produce papers that are attractive objects in their own right, to display in a frame or perhaps use as unusual covers for books.

Watermarks

A watermark is built into a sheet of paper by means of a raised design attached to the mesh of the mould. There is plenty of scope for experiment here. To incorporate a monogram, try using aluminium wire, thick fuse, fishing line or a length of guitar string sewn onto the mesh with very fine thread.

Colouring

You can add food colouring, fabric dyes or water-based paints or inks to the vat to change the colour of the pulp. Analine leather dyes are also worth trying. Always wear rubber gloves when colouring in this way. Another approach is to recycle strongly coloured paper and add this to the pulp.

Bear in mind that the wet pulp will be much darker than the paper when it is dry. The only way to judge the colour of the finished sheet is to make a test piece. A quick way to do this is to take a large pinch of wet pulp, squeeze out the excess water, and either leave the pulp to dry on a radiator, or dry it with a hair-dryer.

Whatever medium you are using, add it to the pulp in gradual stages. Cold-water dyes, powder paints and very concentrated dyes should be added to the base materials in the liquidizer before pulping to ensure that they mix in evenly. Dr Martins dyes (available from artists' suppliers) and fabric dyes should be used particularly sparingly. If the pulp has stained more vividly than you intended, you can add more cotton linters or light-coloured pulp to correct the result. Remember always wear rubber gloves when you are working with colourings, even those that are water-soluble.

Patchworking

A large sheet that combines different colours can be formed by patchworking small sheets together. The sheets are formed without the deckle, so the edges are very ragged, and quite thin.

The first sheet is laid onto a piece of felt and the second sheet is laid next to it, so that the feathered edges overlap. Ideally they should overlap without any ridges or lumps being formed.

Any number of sheets can be joined together. Although it isn't necessary to press the finished sheet before drying, pressing will help to knit the fibres together, thus strengthening the joint.

Dispensing with the deckle means that it is no longer necessary to stick to the rectangular format of the frame. You can partially dip the frame into the pulp, to form narrow strips or triangular corner pieces. Many unusual and striking patterns can be created in this way. Texture can be added by pushing the wet pulp around on the mould before drying.

Other materials can be collaged onto a newly formed sheet by using pulp as an adhesive. Thin sheets of paper, for example, can be held by little blobs of pulp carefully positioned with tweezers. Heavier or bulkier items, such as feathers or string, would need to be held on with thin strips of pulp.

You can laminate different materials between two thin sheets of paper placed one on top of the other before they are dry. This kind of "sandwich" can then be manipulated in various ways. For example, if you laminate string in this way, then pull it away so that it tears through the top layer, you will create interestingly textured ridges along the sheet.

The paper sheets that make up this collage were left to dry before being anchored to each other by tiny pieces of paper pulp, which are almost invisible in the final result. Some of the papers were dyed to create a mottled appearance which improves the overall effect of the piece.

Sandwiching delicate objects such as feathers between two sheets of paper opens up a wealth of creative options. When embedded in a screen, through which light passes, the sand- wiched objects will appear as silhouettes, as in the example illustrated here. However, when the paper is not backlit in this way, the object will show only as a variation of texture. To reveal delicate tex- tures, the paper must be made thin.

Tearing string through paper before it is dry creates novel decorative effects. In the right-hand example here, string threads were pulled through the upper layer of a paper sandwich while the pulp was still wet. Tearing when the pulp is almost dry (left) creates a more ragged edge.

THE PAPER SAMPLER

Needlework samplers were traditionally used to experiment with and perfect different stitches. You can take a similar approach to paper, trying out various techniques to create decorative effects.

The section that follows is a portfolio of paper samplers, designed to introduce you to the repertoire of basic paper skills. Natural-toned papers are used to allow the eye to take in the subtle effects without distraction.

You could assemble a panel of your experiments as a decorative reminder, or simply use the samplers to extend your understanding of the way paper behaves. Try various thicknesses and sizes of paper: they will handle quite differently.

The aim is to provide a starting-point for your imagination, not a set of rigid rules. Once you are familiar with the essential skills, you can use them for more complicated projects, like those described on pages 95-131.

The equipment you will need changes little from one technique to another. For cutting, use a sharp knife or scalpel with a thick card or synthetic cutting mat to preserve your work surface. The pencils you use for marking paper should have a consistent point dimension: it's preferable to use propelling pencils, which need no sharpening. Leads should be H or HB as softer ones smudge. Dividers are useful for marking off equal measurements.

It is worth acquiring a bone folder – that is, a flat piece of bone or plastic with one curved and one pointed (but not sharp) end. This is invaluable for creasing, folding, smoothing and modelling paper, and can be bought from suppliers of bookbinding equipment. Bone is more pleasant to handle than plastic. The folder can be sandpapered easily to shape if the pointed end is too thick. An alternative approach is to adapt an old paperknife or use the blunt edge of a table knife.

Pressing boards are essential. Use two boards of plywood or medium-density fibre-board. The surfaces should be very well sanded to prevent unwanted textures from being impressed into the paper. Waterproof sheets (waxed paper or polythene) will keep the pressing boards dry. When piercing or pressing you will need a soft surface – for example, an old blanket, felt or roughly ½-inch (1cm) thick foam. This should be in two pieces, each one larger than your paper.

Do not apply unnecessary pressure to the paper when you are working, or you will bruise it and make shiny patches. Be sure to select a comfortable working height to prevent back or neck ache. Follow common-sense safety rules when cutting.

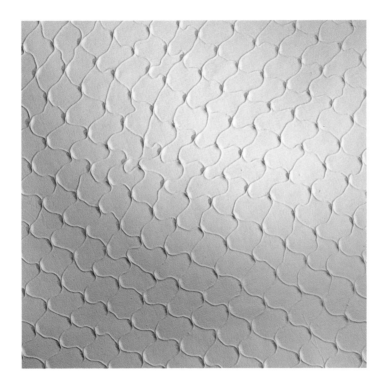

CRUMPLING & CREASING

You will need:
Pressing boards and weights
Old blanket, felt or foam
Waterproof sheets

Crumpled paper may suggest the contents of the waste bin, but you can make surprisingly beautiful textures by crumpling, contrasting well with more ordered techniques. It is also a good way to let off steam!

Take a sheet of paper (not too thick or it will crack) and crumple it firmly. Open out and repeat. The more you do this, the creases become finer and the paper becomes softer. Smooth the sheet out gently.

To add a touch of colour to creased paper, try dipping the crumpled ball into a bowl of warm, diluted coffee or tea for a minute or two. (Later, alter the strength of the solution, or perhaps try cold water fabric dyes.) Allow the ball to dry, then open out fully. Where the fibres have been disturbed by creasing, they will have absorbed more stain than the smooth patches, yielding a crackle finish.

You can give paper a crinkled surface by immersing it in water and allowing it to dry until damp but no longer wet. Flatten it out (not too firmly) and lay it between pressing boards and waterproof sheets to dry, with a heavy weight placed on top. For a more pronounced surface, press with old blankets, felt or foam on top. The paper shrinks as it dries, the creases folding over themselves under pressure, creating little random ridges which retain their texture very well when pasted onto something else.

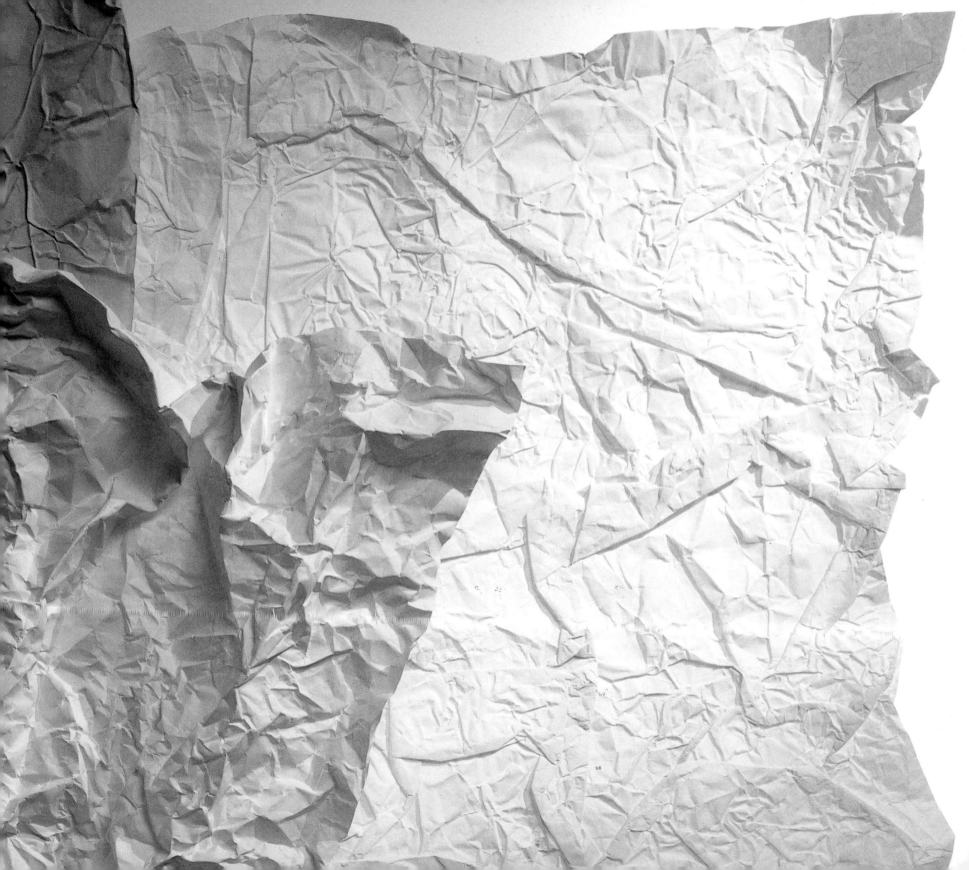

CUTTING & TEARING

You will need:
Sharp knife or scalpel
Cutting mat
Straight edge

The key to successful cutting is a good sharp blade. Don't neglect safety: always use a cutting mat; never cut directly towards yourself; keep fingers well back on the straight edge to avoid accidents.

Many people cut incorrectly, so it's worth spelling out the obvious. Hold the paper firmly down on the mat with the straight edge. Keeping the blade slanted at a constant angle, pull to right or left – not too hard, or you'll drag the paper.

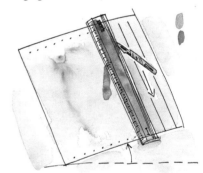

After cutting, don't move the straight edge at once: you may need a second stroke to penetrate. For tightly curved shapes use a smaller blade, such as a tiny dissecting knife or stencil-cutting knife.

Torn shapes have an air of spontaneity and can be unexpectedly intricate. To make regular strips, tear along the grain; tearing across will produce a random, ragged effect.

FOLDING

You will need:
Cutting mat
Pencil or dividers
Straight edge
Bone folder

You need to work precisely to obtain clean, well-formed folds. Determine the grain direction and lay the paper on the cutting mat. Mark out spaces at top and bottom, and if necessary half way down. Divider holes will show through, and are thus more convenient than pencil marks, which have to be made both sides. They are also cleaner.

For each fold, draw the bone folder along the straight edge towards you, pressing down slightly. Fold along the indented line, using a ruler or table edge as a guide, as shown below.

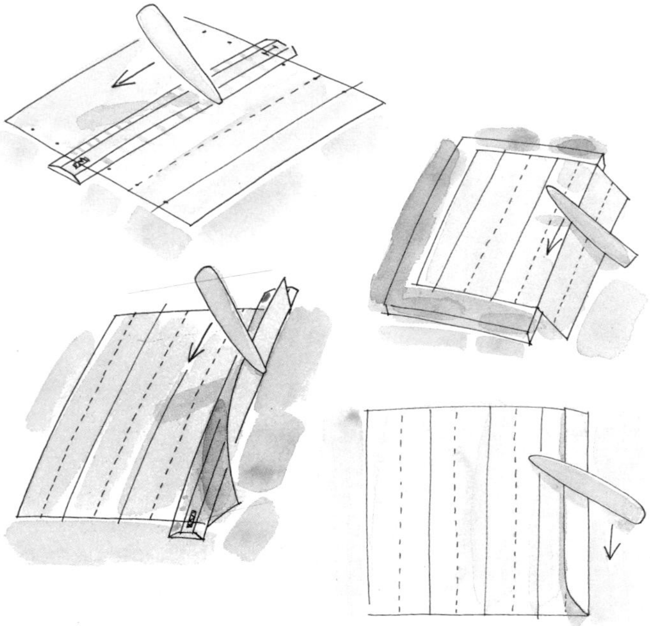

Then reinforce each fold by smoothing the bone folder firmly over it. Turn the sheet over and make the folds on this side similarly (following fresh marks if using a pencil).

FLUTING

You will need:
Stiff paper or card
Thinner paper for the flutes
Paperclips, small bulldog clips
  or clothes pegs
Pencil or dividers
Straight edge
Bone folder
PVA adhesive (see pages 96-7)

Soft folds, or flutes, can suggest the fullness of drapery. To prevent the flutes from straightening out, you must fix them to a support of stiff paper or card. Clips will give a good idea of the effects you can achieve, but use glue for permanence. Try different paper thicknesses.

Mark out the widths on your paper as for folding (see page 50), but judging the intervals so that flat sections (which can be relatively narrow) alternate with sections wide enough for a soft loop fold.

Make your creases as before, but all on the same side of the paper. Reinforce each one by bending the paper up against the straight edge and folding over firmly.

Clip the flat, narrow strips onto the second, stiff sheet of paper. Manipulate the spacing to form either tight loops or gentler humped ridges.

PIERCING

You will need:
*Sewing or knitting needles, hole punches,
    dressmakers' tracing wheels or other
    pointed implements*
Old blanket, felt or piece of old carpet

Perforations can create dramatic changes of
texture across a piece of paper. Light raked
across pierced paper will form interesting
shadows, and you can also exploit backlight-
ing effects, as in traditional punched tin-
work.

  You can use almost any sharp tool. Particularly effective are the hole punches normally used for leather work; for a more
ragged edge, knitting needles are suitable, or
even pencils. When using pointed objects,
place the paper on a yielding surface, such as
blanket or felt, which will create a more
distinct texture on the reverse. The base of a
wire tray is helpful as a guide for making a
grid pattern. If you fold the paper into a
concertina shape, you can make a regularly
spaced pattern with a hole punch or paper
punch which will cut through several sheets
at a time.

SLITTING & SLOTTING

You will need:
Sharp knife or scalpel
Straight edge
Cutting mat
Dividers

It is astonishing how effective a pattern can be made with simple short cuts. Try this with a scalpel or very sharp pointed blade and then hold the paper up against the light. You can then go on to more sophisticated kinds of slitting, and with practice you will soon master the art of creating patterns of flaps, like those shown in the photograph.

Controlled cuts made at regular intervals allow you to thread strips of paper through to give a woven effect, as shown below. Use a cutting mat and avoid putting the cuts too close together or the sheet may fall apart. To allow for the thickness of the paper you may need two cuts for each insert, creating a series of narrow rectangular slits through which the strip is threaded to create a weave.

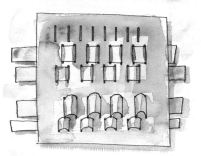

IMPRESSING

You will need:
Dried beans, rice, string, plastic netting
or other suitable objects or textures
Pressing boards, either with weights or with
a press
Old blanket or felt
Waterproof sheets

A plain surface can be textured or patterned
if you press a firm object hard onto the
paper, or if you lay the paper over patterned
or textured materials, such as netting, and
press as hard as possible onto that. With
enough pressure, the paper will take on the
pattern even when dry, but it is often better
to dampen the paper first, so that the fibres
stretch and then shrink again around the
relief surface.

A bookbinder's press, or an old copy press,
will give you the best results. Otherwise you
can improvise with a vice or an old mangle.
Very heavy weights or a firm roller can
produce good results, but you must take care
to apply the pressure evenly.

When using the pressing boards, protect
the lower board against damp with a waterproof sheet and arrange or sprinkle your
rice, beans, netting or whatever on this.
Damp (not soak) the paper and place it on
top of the arrangement. Cover with a blanket
and place the other pressing board on top.
Press beneath heavy weights for an hour or
more until the paper is dry.

If you want to make several impressions
from one design, you can glue objects onto
strong paper or card to make a permanent
block. Experiment with different types of
paper – the pattern tends to last longer on
thicker papers. Handmade papers are particularly effective but not essential.

WEAVING

You will need:
Sharp knife and straight edge
Cutting mat
Pencil or dividers
Stiff board
Adhesive tape

Complex patterns can be built up by weaving. You can use either cut or torn papers, and you can vary the width and angles of the crossways (weft) strips and upright (warp) ones. Plain, coloured or patterned papers can be introduced.

  Divide a sheet of paper with measured widths, as described for folding (page 50). Use the marks to guide your straight edge and, starting about ½in (1cm) down from the top, cut the paper into a fringe.

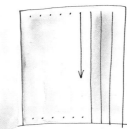

Cut along the grain, as this will provide a more rigid support for weaving. Tape the uncut length onto a stiff board.

  Cut strips from another sheet of paper, across the grain for flexibility. After you have woven three or four strips across, the warp strips will begin to splay at the lower end. They can be kept parallel by cutting through the retaining strip – the first few wefts will now hold everything in place.

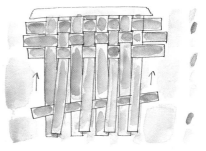

DECORATING PAPER

Papers have been decorated by hand for centuries, and the same historic methods can be followed today with equal success. A trip to a museum with a decorative arts collection can be a rewarding source of ideas for patterns. However, even though the techniques are traditional, you need not be tied to the past or the exotic in your quest for motifs – modern textiles, wall coverings, even the patterns in nature, can suggest eye-catching treatments. And, of course, there is plenty of scope for experiment: you can be as flamboyant or as abstract as you wish.

It is exciting to go to a good paper supplier's and choose from the range of decorative papers available – especially if they are made and patterned by hand. Still more rewarding – and not so expensive – is to create your own unique patterns on paper. There are various decorative techniques that you can follow to make interesting shapes, lines and colours that fascinate the eye. You can decorate paper to create a surface that is pleasing enough in its own right to display on a wall, perhaps in a suitable frame, or to

use as gift wrapping paper. Or you can treat decoration as merely the first step in creating something more lasting – such as jewelry, a decorative box or tray, a covering for a book – even wallpaper.

The methods described over the following pages are all intended as starting points for experiment. They demand little in the way of equipment, and can be followed very easily even by people who have never had any experience. Success in decorating paper depends largely on the imaginative use of colour and pattern. Generally, the more simple the approach, the more effective. There are no precise rules, but there *are* a few basic guidelines with which you should familiarize yourself before you begin. They are described in the pages on pattern-making, which begin this section.

If your first attempts at pattern-making seem forced, do not be discouraged. Many people feel awkward to begin with, and this has an adverse effect on the results. In time you will gain in self-confidence, and be able to create more spontaneous, natural-looking designs.

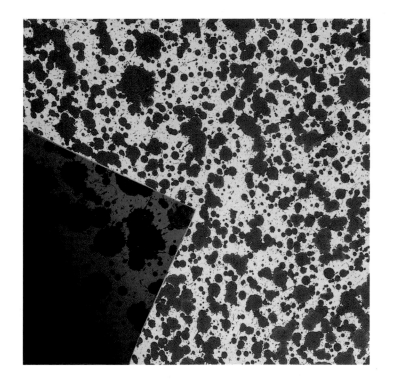

PRINCIPLES OF PATTERN MAKING

A pattern may be made by drawing marks, by texturing the paper surface or by spontaneous effects created in a variety of ways. As with other aspects of papercraft, there are no precise rules. You can decorate a sheet of paper with random flamboyance, or at the other end of the scale you can create a controlled effect based on repetition. Between the two extremes there are various degrees of control.

Repeat patterns are ideal for paper that will be used for covering an object. The size of the repeated motifs should be scaled according to the paper's intended use.

There are certain guidelines you can follow, serving as a basis for all kinds of repeat designs. Use graph paper to practise if you find that this helps.

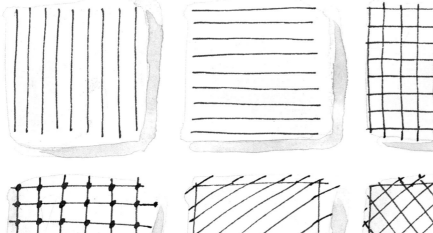
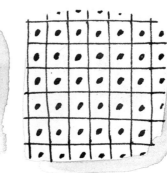
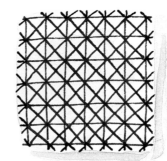

These simple variations on a limited range of pattern-making themes are intended merely as launching pads for your own ideas. Note how the slight irregularities inevitable with freehand drawing add character to the designs.

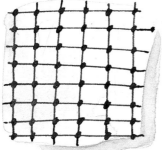
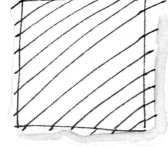
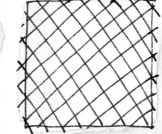

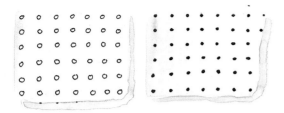

The simplest repeat pattern is the repeat grid, within which even simple dots, as shown above, can be varied in their effect by altering their size and the way in which they are made.

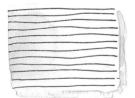

By alternating solid dots with circles as shown above, you can create an overall effect of stripes or set up movement in a diagonal direction.

Lines, drawn either with a ruler or freehand, offer plenty of decorative scope. By breaking them up or incorporating a wobble, as above, you can vary their impact.

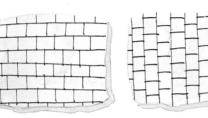

A half-drop repeat, like that of a brick wall, adds movement and interest. Try using the half-drop pattern as a grid for a series of simple motifs, like the circles shown in the diagram above. These need not be intricately drawn.

Contrast is important to the liveliness of a pattern. The counterpoint may be between large and small, solid and linear, thick and thin, precise and uneven, dark and light, close and open, busy and quiet.

Colour, of course, is an essential element in decorating paper. It lends excitement and impact to pattern. However, unless you have very strong convictions about colour, it might be helpful to work initially within a limited colour range.

One colour on different coloured papers will give ample variety. Black on white paper, and white on black, yield surprisingly different effects. With some decorative techniques, you can apply colours side by side, and some cross-mixing will occur to produce other colours on the overlaps.

Remember that there will usually be enough variation in the paint to create tonal interest, from light to dark — all the more reason to restrict your colour palette to one, two or three hues.

Sometimes it will take only a small amount of a strong colour to animate a background of contrasting hue. Use warm, sunny colours to set off colder blues and greens, and vice versa.

PASTE AND COLOUR

This ancient method of decorating is beautifully simple. First you make a mixture of starch paste and a pigment and spread it over a sheet of paper. You then work into the mixture in its wet state, patterning or texturing it by drawing or printing onto it. The variations of thickness create effects that are surprisingly three-dimensional.

One colour is enough to create an interesting pattern, but it is also possible to use two or three colours. However, the colours will mix, so if you use too many they may end up looking muddy.

A paste made from plain white flour and water gives good results. Use 3 ounces (85g) of flour to 1 pint (½ litre) of cold water. Mix the flour to a paste in the water and allow to stand for a half-hour or more. Then gradually bring to the boil, stirring constantly. You should use a stainless steel pan – or best of all, a glass bowl in a pan of water. The latter method will prevent burning, although it is slower. Don't use ferrous metal pans or chipped enamel containers, as any iron will eat through paper. Cook for ten minutes. Cool before use. The paste should be the consistency of (unwhipped) double cream – a little runnier if you are using powder paints. If the paste seems too thick, add cold water. Do not keep the paste for more than a day or two or it will go off.

Powder paints, poster paints and watercolour printing inks all work well. Your paper should not be too thin or it may tear as you work it. Nor should it be too absorbent, or glossy. Cartridge papers are ideal for the purpose.

Mix a strong colour with a pot or jam jar of paste until you think it is dark enough – bearing in mind that colours turn a little paler as they dry. Experiment with different ratios of paste to colour. The two basic methods of applying the colour and pattern to the paper are described below (methods one and two). Method three describes more precise pattern-making with a piece of card

instead of a sponge or brush; you could equally well use any other pointed, cut or serrated edge.

When dry, the patterned paper will be curled and dimpled where the paste has contracted, but will become quite flat when pasted onto a surface – or, in the meantime, you can flatten it between two pressing boards with a weight on top. After decorating one sheet, thoroughly clean the work surface before working on another sheet.

Method 1: paste on paper
Place the paper on the work surface and lay a thick trail of colour/paste along one edge. Working from this side, use a wide brush to spread the mix evenly and fairly thickly over the entire surface.

Using a sponge or brush, stipple evenly across the colour. The more you practise, the more you will be able to control the pressure and direction to obtain the effect you want. Finally, peel off the paper and lay it on newspaper to dry. The pattern below is typical of the effects you can achieve by this method.

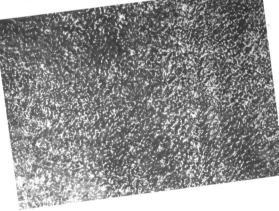

Method 2: paper on paste
Paste up the work surface over an area larger than your sheet of paper. Stipple with a sponge or brush to create a pattern.

Lay the paper onto the surface and smooth lightly over the back with a soft cloth. Then peel off the paper from the surface, starting with one corner. This method produces a characteristic softness, as shown in the example below: compare this with the paste on paper method illustrated in the previous column.

Method 3: using card
Place the paper on the work surface and paste up all over (as with method one). Take a strip of card about as long as a pencil; the width is not critical, but you could try 1 inch (2.5cm) to start with. Pull this down or across the sheet in a zig-zag movement. Repeat to form a pattern. The example below was made by this method.

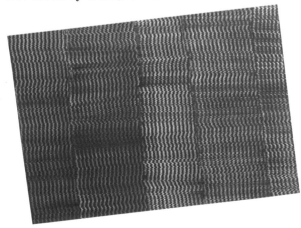

You will need:

Starch paste
Water-mixable pigments – for example,
watercolours, powder paints
Sheets of cartridge paper or similar
Bowl and saucepan for mixing paste
Jars and mixing spoons – one for each
colour
Assorted household paint brushes
Sponges, rags, rolled paper, stiff card and
other objects for pattern-making
Easily wiped work surface – for example, a
formica top or plate glass
Rags for cleaning up
Newspapers on which to dry papers
Pressing boards and weights for flattening

With the paste and colour method, you can make effective patterns with flat pieces of card, whether rectangular or comb-shaped as illustrated above right. Moving the comb in a wavy line without altering its angle creates interesting variations of thickness. Twisting a rectangular piece of card around a central point makes a bow-tie shape. The photograph at right shows marks made with cards of different shapes.

There are countless pattern-making tech-niques for use with the paste and colour method. Try natural hand movements for a freehand or callig-raphic effect, or make simple stripes or waves using a comb or piece of card with a serrated edge. Dabbing objects onto the paper treated with paste and colour creates a ghosted image. You could experiment with superimposing two or three layers of colour, decorating one layer and allowing it to dry before adding the next layer and decorating that in turn. Or you could place a mask on the paper and work paste/colour over it; then peel off the mask to leave a space for the second colour or a frame around the edge of the pattern.

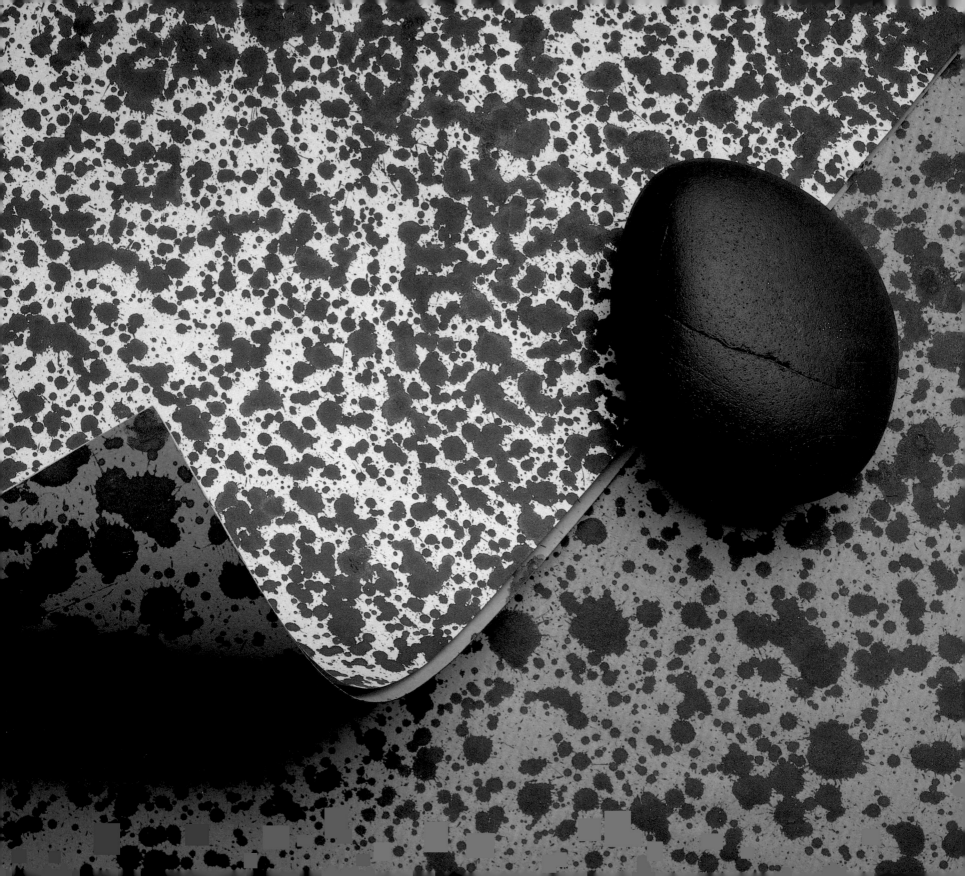

SPATTERING AND SPRAYING

You will need:
*Old stiff brushes – for example, tooth-
    brushes or paintbrushes – or an atomizer
    or airbrush*
Stiff card or blunt knife for use with a brush
Cartridge paper or similar
Masking tape
Paint masking fluid (optional)
*Paint jars, and shallow dishes for wider
    brushes*
A large cardboard box
Lots of newspapers

The only drawback to these quick and easy methods is that they can be messy. For this reason, washable, water-based pigments are preferable to waterproof inks or cold water dyes. A large cardboard box makes a useful shield: either put your paper in the box while spattering onto it, or cut the box up and use the pieces to make a protective surround to your working area. Use sheets of newspaper as further protection. Large-scale work is best done outdoors – water-based colours will wash away fairly quickly and will not harm grass or plants.

Spattering with a stiff brush
Dip the tip of the bristles into a colour. Take care not to pick up too much colour at once or it will fall in blobs. Hold the brush over one edge of the paper and then move it across the whole area while firmly stroking across the bristles with the edge of a piece of card or blunt knife (towards you – or you will spatter yourself!). Recharge the brush as necessary. After the colour is dry, add another colour if desired.

Spraying
An atomizer (as shown below) or airbrush will produce a fine spray for more regular effects.

Fix the paper onto a board (such as a formica top) and prop the board at a slant. Load the airbrush or atomizer with colours that have an ink-like consistency – any lumps may block the equipment. Spray the colours onto the paper. Immediately lay the board flat to prevent the colours from running.

An airbrush is an expensive item but gives more control once you have mastered the art of using it. Altering the distance from the

nozzle to the paper allows you to vary the effect. You can also adjust the flow rate by altering the pressure on the control button. After using an airbrush, it's essential to clean it properly. Empty the reservoir and refill with clean water. Then press the button to squirt water through the nozzle. Remove any specks of paint from the nozzle and reservoir using a hog's hair brush – don't use a brush with very fine bristles or they might lodge unobserved in the equipment. Finally, dismantle the airbrush very carefully, and rub any traces of colour from the central needle. Apply a little vaseline to the needle – or run it through your hair – to keep it functioning smoothly.

*Left: Spattering boldly,
with big brushes, lots
of paint and wide open
spaces between the
blobs, creates a
dramatic pattern like
that of a bird's speck-
led egg.*

Using a mask

Masking off an area of the paper with stencils while spattering allows you to create overlapping effects of one-, two- and three-colour pattern.

Spatter a sheet of paper as described on the previous page. When the colour is dry, lay strips of paper over the pattern. Spatter the second colour onto the first. When the second colour is dry, lift off the strips.

Try arranging the strips in different positions to create chequered effects. Experiment with torn or cut shapes.

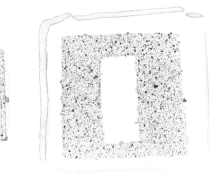

An alternative method of masking, giving a less precise effect, is to paint masking fluid (from an art supplier) over the paper after a layer of colour is dry; then spatter more colour; and when the second layer is dry, gently rub off the masking fluid. The fluid may take off a little colour with it, making it slightly paler.

Cumulative spraying using masks works best when the mask shapes are simple. The right-hand paper here has been given three applications of paint. To begin with, pink was sprayed over the whole black paper surface. Then, rectangular masks were arranged in different positions for the second and third coats of white and blue. The palest areas have received all three layers.

An airbrush allows more controlled effects than an atomizer, but you will need to practise long and hard to achieve an even finish. You can adjust the texture of the spray from coarse to fine, as desired. The chequerboard pattern here was created by folding the paper into squares and airbrushing each folded-up square in turn. By crinkling paper and spraying obliquely from one side you can capture a three-dimensional effect when the sheet is flattened out again, as shown by the other example photographed here (near right). As a less expensive alternative to an airbrush, you could use a modelmaker's spray kit, incorporating a can of compressed air.

RESIST PATTERN AND COLOUR WASH

These techniques are similar in effect to stencilling, although the method of working is freer. You create patterns by masking parts of the paper with wax, masking fluid or process white paint, then washing colour over the surface, leaving the masked area unaffected. Use fairly strong paper.

Wax method

You will need:
Candle
Watercolour paints, or inks
Card, paper or a textured surface to form the pattern
Masking tape
Large paint brush and jars for mixing
Newspapers for drying

Lay the paper on a textured surface or a pattern of torn or cut shapes of card or paper. Tape down to secure. Then rub the candle firmly across the whole area. Brush the colour evenly across the paper. It will not adhere to the raised waxed areas – only to the spaces between. A negative image of the underlying pattern will be formed.

Left: *Two simple graphic designs made by the masking fluid method.*

Masking fluid method

You will need:
Masking fluid
Ruling pen, dip pen or fine watercolour brush – preferably synthetic
Large paint brush
Colours (as for wax method)
Jars for mixing paints
Cloth for removing masking fluid
Newspapers for drying

Drop, flick, trail, dab or draw a pattern of masking fluid onto the paper with a pen or brush. When the fluid is dry, brush or spray colour over the paper. When the colour is dry, gently rub the surface with a cloth or with your hand to remove the thin rubbery layer of masking fluid. Follow the same procedure to apply a second colour, if desired.

This method, and to a lesser degree the process white method that follows, is especially suitable if you want to make a design that includes fine lines. The edges of the pattern are crisper than you can achieve with the wax method, which is suitable for softer effects.

Process white method

You will need:
Designer's process white paint (from art suppliers)
Pen or fine brush for drawing
Assorted brushes
Waterproof inks or designer's tempera colours
Shower attachment or rubber hose – useful for rinsing
Soft cloth or sponge
Household tray or sheet of formica or glass to support paper during washing

The shapes made by this technique will have a slightly softer edge than those made by the masking fluid method.

Place the paper on a washable tray or other hard surface and drop, flick, trail, dab or draw a pattern of process white onto the paper with a pen or brush. When thoroughly dry, brush the entire area with colour.

When the colour is completely dry, rinse the paper under running water, gently wiping with a cloth or sponge or "tickling" with a brush to remove all the process white.

BLOCK PRINTING WITH FOUND OR CUT OBJECTS

Block printing is a classic way to apply a repeated pattern. An object whose surface has been inked up is pressed firmly onto a sheet of paper to create a mirror image of the object's shape or design. You can either cut into the object to create the printing surface or you can use it as it is.

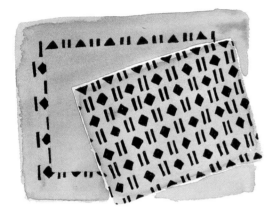

Your aim should be to make the printed paper look as if it has been cut out of a larger sheet of the same pattern. Beginners tend to start inside the confines of the paper, which is wrong. Instead, you should take two adjacent sides and overlap them with the first rows of the printed pattern, as shown above.

Perhaps the most familiar type of block printing is the potato cut. But many other materials can equally well be cut into – some, such as lino and wood, requiring special cutting tools. Rubber erasers are easily cut into suitable blocks. The plastic types do not absorb the ink well enough – unless you roughen the surface with the finest grade of sandpaper.

Using found objects

You will need:
Corks, wooden buttons, leaves or other suitable objects
Water- or oil-based inks
Turpentine or white spirits (for oil-based inks)
Palette knife or flexible kitchen knife
Rollers of different widths
Glass or formica sheet
Rags and newspapers Rubber gloves

When selecting a suitable object, ensure that the printing surface is smooth and on one plane. If the object is small, you can glue it to a length of doweling or a wood block to make handling easier.

Put on rubber gloves before you start to ink. Apply a little ink to the inking plate and smooth out with a palette knife. Push the roller back and forth and at right angles several times to ink it evenly. Then pass the

roller over the surface of the object until it too is evenly coated. Keeping the block at a right angle to the paper, press firmly and steadily downwards. Lift without smudging.

If you are using a leaf for printing, ink it and place it on the paper with a newspaper on top. Roll with a clean roller, then lift the newspaper and the leaf. Repeat using a fresh

sheet of wastepaper each time. Alternatively, ink up several leaves to form the pattern and roll all at the same time. Oil-based inks are best for inking up a number of printing surfaces, as water-based ones tend to dry out too quickly.

Using eraser blocks

You will need:
Rubber eraser block
Sharp knife or scalpel
Soft pencil
Water- or oil-based printing inks
White spirit or turpentine
Palette knife or kitchen knife
Cutting mat
Rollers of different widths
Glass or formica sheet
Rags and newspapers
Rubber gloves

Draw a simple design onto the eraser with a soft pencil. On the cutting mat, cut the design into the block, angling the blade so that the printing surfaces have outwardly sloping sides: this makes the block stronger. You should not cut too deep – just enough to prevent the design from infilling with ink. Neither should you make the cut lines too close, or the pattern will crumble. When you are satisfied with the pattern, ink and print as above.

Right: *Block printing is highly versatile. The central sheet here is black paper sprayed with white ink, then printed in blue and black using blocks of wood. The front and back examples were printed from pieces of cut cardboard pasted onto paper. Behind the half-moon paper is one printed from a sheet on which torn strips of paper were stuck.*

MONOTYPE

You will need:

Pencils, knitting needles or any other objects for making decorative marks
Printing inks (preferably oil-based)
White spirit or turpentine (with oil-based inks)
Sheet of glass
Palette knife
Rollers and inking plate (direct method)
Rags and newspapers
Rubber gloves

This is a simple one-print-at-a-time technique – although with practice you can repeat patterns. The quality can be similar to that of paste and colour methods, but with less of the three-dimensional effect.

The procedure is as follows. First, ink up the glass all over, using the palette knife and roller. Use one colour initially – later you can go on to try patches of different colours. Lay the paper down smoothly and without pressure to make contact with the ink. Using your chosen object, draw or press the pattern on the back of the paper, perhaps varying the width of the lines or the amount of pressure. Then peel off the paper. The lines will have a softened appearance, as though drawn with a

soft crayon. The background texture will be pleasingly speckled.

There is an alternative approach to monotype printing, whereby the pattern is drawn directly onto the glass instead of on the paper. If you paint onto the glass with a dilute ink, whether oil- or water-based, the effect will be more fluid, probably with

spreading of the edges. Ink up the glass and work into the ink as you would with the paste and colour mix (see page 66). Then lay the paper on the glass. Smooth over it with a clean roller. Finally, peel off the paper.

Opposite: *A patchwork of patterns made by the monotype method. The glass was inked up with black ink and then drawn into with strips of card and pointed objects, including spent ballpoint pens. The spotty effects were made by removing areas of ink from the glass and then putting on blobs of ink in a pattern. Only the square at bottom right was left unpatterned: here, when the paper was laid over the glass, squiggly marks were made by lightly pressing a blunt instrument onto the surface. Finally, a roller was run over the paper. With the monotype method, the depth of colour transferred can be altered by varying the pressure at this stage.*

MARBLING

Marbling is a technique of decorating paper using colours floated on a liquid. The patterns thus formed are then transferred to a sheet of paper. Many of the easiest patterns to form have a wavy and veined appearance, resembling real marble. This is how marbling has acquired its name.

The origins of the craft are not precisely known, but are certainly to be found in the East. In ancient times, perhaps as early as the 8th century, the Japanese wrote on paper which was delicately marbled in one area. Marbling was popular in Persia and Turkey, appearing as decoration on miniatures and calligraphic manuscripts in the 16th century. Marbled papers were also used to line boxes, which found their way to Europe. By the 17th century so-called "Dutch work" was shipped to England wrapped around small items such as toys, as a strategem for escaping the heavy duty on imported papers. On arrival the paper was carefully removed, flattened and then sold – mainly to bookbinders.

The marbling process was for a long time a closely guarded secret. Even apprentices were taught only separate stages of the craft – not the entire procedure.

Today there continues to be a certain reluctance to divulge all the secrets of the more sophisticated marbling techniques. However, there are various basic approaches that can be mastered with surprising ease. And there is plenty of room for experiment.

The easiest way to marble paper is to exploit the reaction of oil and water, which don't mix. Any of the methods using oil paints are virtually foolproof, and ideal for beginners. Different types and densities of size (that is, the liquid on which the colours sit), and different thicknesses and combinations of colours, will produce interesting and varied results.

The classic marbling method, also described in the pages that follow, is a little more complex but still well within the reach of a determined beginner. The technique involves floating watercolours on a gelatinous size made from caragheen moss (Irish seaweed). Ox-gall is added to the colours to make them spread out and prevent them from sinking. When you lift the paper off the moss mixture, bits of size remain clinging to it. These need to be washed away, but you can only do this if you treat the paper before you start with a solution of alum, to ensure that the colours are not all washed away with the size.

SIMPLE MARBLING

You will need:

*Container to hold the water: for example, a
photographer's tray or washing-up bowl*
Small jars or pots to mix the colours in
*Needles, small sticks (for example, cocktail
sticks), paint brushes or drinking straws
(for manipulating the colours)*
Pipette or eye dropper
*Lots of newspapers – or an indoor drying
line*
Oil paints
Turpentine or white spirit

Some lovely patterns can be created simply
by floating oil colours on water – there is no
need to make up a special size. This is the
easiest of all the marbling methods. All the
paints should be mixed with white spirit, or
turpentine, until they will shake easily from
the brush – but are not too runny. Mix all
the colours to more or less the same
thickness.

The paper you use should be trimmed to
slightly smaller than your tray. Any colour of
cartridge paper or drawing paper is suitable,
but it is a good idea to start with white so that
you can see your patterns easily.

Fill the container with water to a depth of
around 3–4in (7.5–10cm). Flick drops of
colour over the water with a drop brush,
distributing them fairly evenly – or spread
over the water surface with a pipette. The
drops should spread to about 1–2in
(2.5–5cm) in diameter. If they don't, the
colour is too thick: add more white spirit or
turps. If the drops spread out quickly and
break up, the colour is too thin: add more
paint. If the drops expand slightly and then
shrink, the water may be too warm: add
more cold water.

After applying the colours, the next step is
to make the pattern. Don't try to make this
too regular. One method is to blow the
colours gently over the water surface with a
drinking straw. Or alternatively, you could
swirl them around with a needle, thin stick

or the handle of a small paint brush. If the
colours sink slightly during vigorous stirring, they will always float back to the
surface. However, the longer you stir, the
more the colours will mix, perhaps becoming "muddy". The thinner the paint, the
sooner this happens.

The basic method of transferring your
patterns onto a sheet of paper is very simple.
It applies to whatever kind of marbling you
are doing – from this failsafe beginner's
method to the more advanced techniques
described over the following pages. Take
hold of diagonally opposite corners of the
sheet, holding them slightly in from the
width of the paper, so that it hangs in a
gentle curve (see diagram on page 87).
Carefully lower this curve into the centre of
the water, and gently push down and out
towards the edges until the whole sheet is in
contact with the surface.

With freeform marbling, air bubbles are
not necessarily a problem. However, they
will form blank spots in the design. If you
want to avoid this effect, the secret is to
lower the paper very carefully so that no air
pockets are created. If you see any appearing,
you may be able to disperse them by lightly
tapping the paper down onto the water
surface.

Lift the sheet out of the tray. To dry it, all
you need to do is leave the sheet, pattern side
up, on a pile of newspaper or hang it on an
indoor drying line.

After making a print there is likely to be a
residue of paint on the water. You can
remove this by pulling a strip of newspaper
across the surface until it is clean. Then you
can make another pattern without having to
refill the tray. If you wish, you can deliberately leave a few bits of colour on the water
so that they make a contribution to the next
pattern.

Making and using a drop brush

Traditionally made from long strands of
camel hair, a drop brush holds a lot of paint
which drops from the brush easily when you
tap it over water. Instead, you can use a
bristle whisk from a kitchen supplies shop.
Or you can make your own drop brush using
drinking straws at least 8in (20cm) long and
some string or rubber bands. Take a batch of
about ten straws and bind them in the
middle: this gives you a 4in (10cm) brush
with a 4in (10cm) handle.

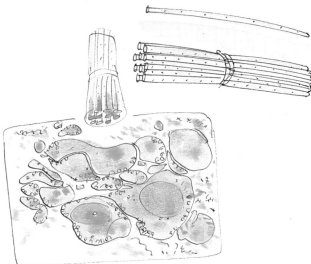

To use the brush dip it in the colour, then
hold it over the water and tap it across the
fingers of your other hand.

*Right: A single colour can be effective, especially
if used on a background sheet of complementary
colour. However, there is no limit to the number
of colours you can use, and they can be as subtle
or vivid as you like.*

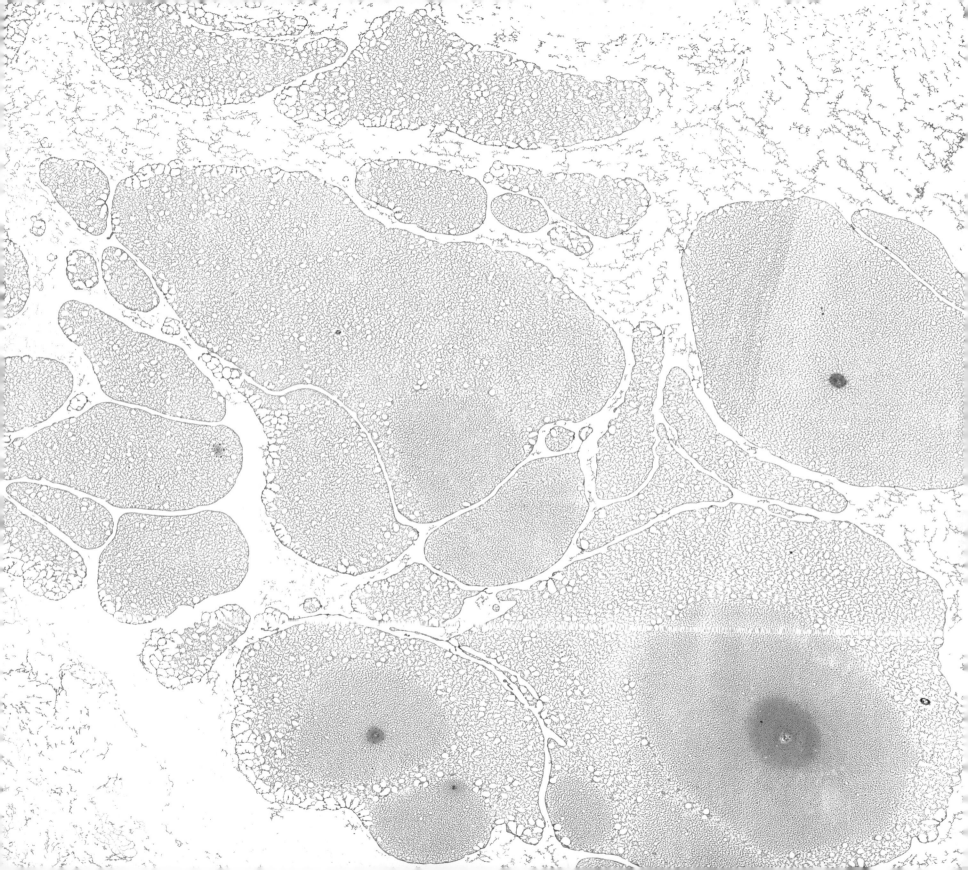

MARBLING ON SIZE

When you marble using oil paints and water, you can *encourage* a particular pattern to form, but you cannot control it precisely. If you want to form more controlled patterns, you need to use a thickened size instead of water as a base on which to float the oils. You can then work more slowly, confident that the pattern won't change while you are preparing to transfer it to the paper. Generally, the thicker the size, the more regular the patterns that can be formed. Wallpaper size offers an easy and inexpensive alternative to water, but there are many other options, which you will find described in specialized books on marbling.

The recipe for wallpaper paste size is as follows:

4 heaped tablespoons of wallpaper paste
9 pints (5 litres) of water at room
temperature

Mix the wallpaper paste with 2 pints (1 litre) of the water, stirring continuously for at least 30 seconds. Add the rest of the water and mix well. Leave to stand for a while, stirring occasionally to ensure that the paste thickens smoothly. You can use it in this thick, sauce-like state, or thin it for looser patterns. However, if made too thin, the size will behave exactly like a water base.

The marbling procedure itself is basically the same as for the failsafe beginners' method, except that you need to wash off any paste from the marbled paper before hanging it up to dry. Bear in mind that you must distribute the paint evenly over the size if you want to achieve a regular pattern.

Once you have mastered the basic technique, you can experiment to see what different effects you can create. For example, try using a mixture of thick and thin paint.

You will need:
Wallpaper paste for the size
Mixing bowl and bucket for making the size
Shallow container – such as a
*   photographer's tray*
Small jars or pots to mix the colour in
Needles, small sticks, paintbrushes or
*   drinking straws to manipulate the colour*
Pipette or eye-dropper
Lots of old newspapers – or indoor drying
*   line*
Newspaper cut into approximately 3in
*   (7.5cm) strips, for cleaning surface of size*
Formica board, or similar – to support
*   paper while washing*
Shower head attachment – or sponge
Oil paints in any colours
Turpentine or white spirit

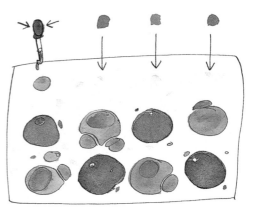

1 *After making the size and mixing the colours apply drops of colour in an all-over pattern with a pipette or drop brush. If the colour expands and then shrinks on the surface, the water is too warm or too cold – experience will enable you to judge which. Add a little hot or cold water to solve the problem. If the colour sinks, the size may be too thick; add more water.*

5a *Lay the sheet pattern side up on a formica board or other firm support and wash gently with a shower attachment to remove any residue of paste.*

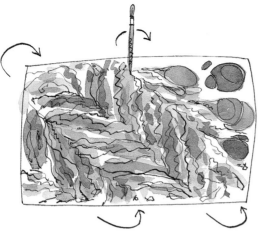

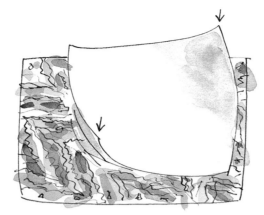

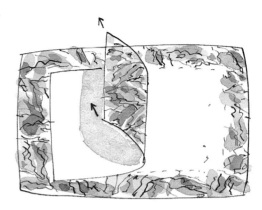

2 *Manipulate the colours with a needle or thin stick, or by blowing through a drinking straw. If you are using two or more colours, remember that they will begin to mix and become "muddy" if you stir for too long – especially if they are quite thinly mixed.*

3 *When you have the pattern you want, lower the paper carefully so that no air bubbles are trapped underneath. Take hold of diagonally opposite corners of the sheet, holding them slightly in from the width of the paper, so that it hangs in a gentle curve. Carefully lower onto the size, pushing the corners down. In effect, you should almost roll the paper out across the surface: do not simply let it fall, or you will create air bubbles.*

4 *Lift the sheet out of the tray in a gentle peeling motion, holding it by the edges.*

5ᵇ *Alternatively, rinse the paper on a formica board under a running tap, sponging the surface with great care to avoid lifting off the pattern as well.*

6 *Dry the paper: either leave the sheet pattern side up on a wadge of newspaper, or hang it on an indoor drying line.*

7 *After making a print there is likely to be a residue of paint on the size. To prepare the tray for re-use, remove the paint by pulling a strip of newspaper across the surface until it is clean. You can then make another pattern on the surface of the size. It is important to keep the size clean, or the colours won't spread. Cover when not in use to prevent dust from accumulating.*

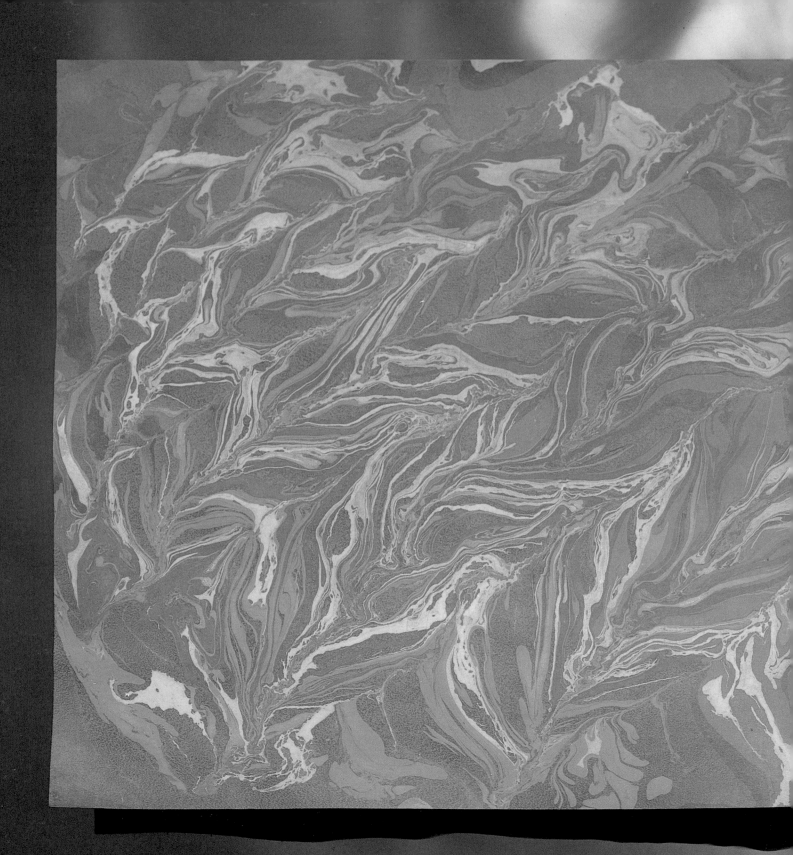

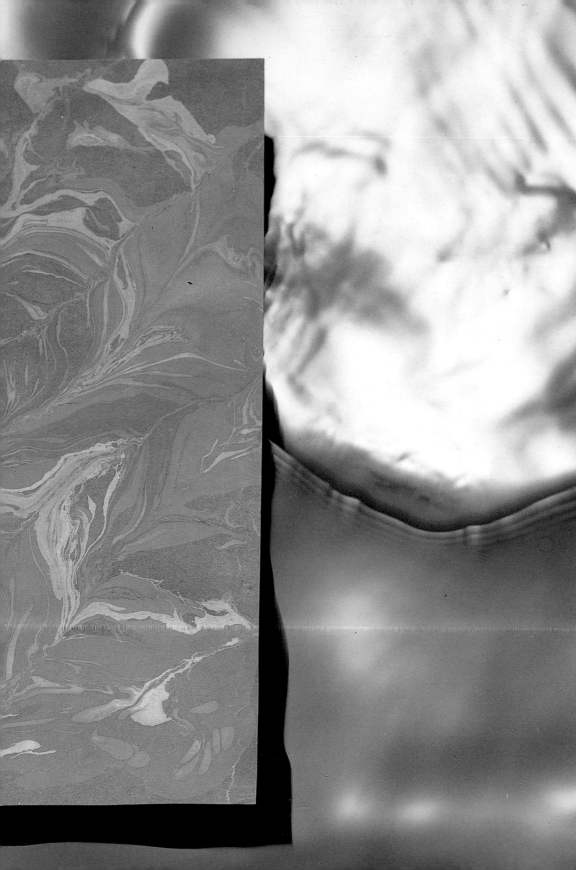

Wallpaper paste makes an excellent and inexpensive size on which you can create marbled patterns that are fluid but not totally freeform. The spreading of the colours is not so great as to distort the basic design. In this example, grey and green have been coaxed into an interlocking pattern with the end of a brush handle.

CLASSIC MARBLING

One of the most familiar traditional marbling styles is a repeating pattern of very fine combed effects. To copy this classic form you will need to use ready-prepared marbling colours, watercolours or gouache on a size of caragheen moss. For best results you need to follow a few simple rules: keep all marbling equipment clean; prepare the size with care; take time testing the colours; and keep everything at room temperature. This last point is crucial. The size works well at a temperature of 60–65°F (15–18°C) – 50°F (10°C) is too cold, 70°F (21°C) too hot.

Caragheen moss is available in dried or powdered forms. The powdered form is available from artists' suppliers; the recipe for making it up as size is given on page 86. However, you may find it easier to buy the moss in its dried form from a health food shop. There are two alternative recipes. Try both to find the one you feel most comfortable with.

If you plan to do marbling in any quantity, you can add formalin or formaldehyde to the size; this will preserve it for about a week or so, as long as you remember to store it in a cold place. Only a few drops per pint (half-litre) of cooled size are needed. Never add these preservatives to hot size, as the fumes are toxic.

Method 1
2½oz (71g) of dried caragheen moss
10 pints (5.7 litres) of water

Add the moss to 8 pints (4.5 litres) of the water in a large saucepan. Put on the stove for about 10 minutes, stirring the mixture when it boils. Remove from heat and add cold water. When the liquid has cooled, pour it through a sieve to remove the residue of seaweed. Leave the size to stand for at least 24 hours until slightly gelatinous. It is then ready for use, although you may find it easier to work with if you add more water.

Method 2
2oz (57g) of dried caragheen moss
8 pints (4.5 litres) of water

Put the moss in a large saucepan with half the water and bring to the boil over a low heat. This should take at least an hour. Allow to boil for three minutes, stirring continually. Remove from the heat and add the rest of the water. Leave overnight or longer. Strain through a sieve. The size is now ready for use. It should feel gelatinous, but still be liquid. The mixture should be clear amber.

Marbling colours should be very finely ground, or they may sink into the size. Ready-prepared colours in liquid form are the most reliable. However, if these are unobtainable, watercolours or gouache paints are good alternatives.

Before marbling you must treat the paper with a mordant – a chemical which makes paper and colour receptive to each other and improves colour fastness.

Whichever type of colours you use, you must mix them with ox-gall. This prevents different colours from mixing together; and, because it reduces the surface tension of the size, it also helps them to spread more evenly. The second colour you add to the size needs more ox-gall than the first, the third more than the second, and so on. Initially it is best to work with just two colours, until you have learned how they behave. Prepare the first colour in a ratio of 6 drops of ox-gall to 2 teaspoons of colour. You must always test each colour before use. If the colour doesn't spread, add a couple more drops of ox-gall. If it still won't spread, add a little distilled water. (Colours can be diluted by as much as twice their original amount in this way.) If this doesn't work, the size may be too thick, in which case you can thin it down with water. If the colours drop through the size, this is another indication that the size is too thick: when the colours can't spread, they sink.

Remember that the temperature of the size can affect the way the colours behave. If the size is too cold, add a little hot water. If too thin, and you don't want to add more water, heat it up in a saucepan and then leave to cool for an hour or so. Skim the surface of the size before you add colours.

Having reached this stage, you are ready to proceed with pattern-making, as described on pages 92–3.

You will need:

Mixing bowl and bucket for mixing up the size

Large saucepan and fine sieve or nylon stocking for preparing and straining size

Shallow container to hold the size: a photographer's tray is ideal

Jug for mixing up alum solution

Small jars or pots to mix colours in

Pipette or eye-dropper

Marbling combs for pattern-making

Lots of old newspapers – or an indoor drying line

Dried caragheen moss or powdered caragheen moss extract or caragheenam (caragheen extract). Most of these can be bought from artists' suppliers but the dried form will be cheaper in health food shops

Sheets of cartridge or other drawing paper cut to slightly smaller than your tray

Prepared marbling colours, watercolours or gouache in tube form

Alum crystals and ox-gall: both available from artists' suppliers

Distilled water

Formalin or formaldehyde. These are preservatives, only needed if you plan to do a lot of marbling. Available from a chemist

Borax. Only needed if your water is very hard. Available from a chemist

Making a marbling comb

Marbling combs can be bought from an artists' supplier. Or you can improvise with an ordinary hair comb with some of the teeth broken off. Alternatively, you can make your own marbling comb – it is worth making several, with variations, for different kinds of pattern. All you need are some card, pins or needles, and contact adhesive.

Cut two pieces of card about 2in (5cm) deep and slightly narrower than the width of the marbling tray. Mark on the card the positions for the pins, measuring carefully to ensure that they are evenly spaced. Pins spaced ⅛in (3 mm) apart will yield a fine comb pattern. For a coarser effect, and for first attempts, increase the spacing. Cut notches deep enough to embed each pin, ensuring that they all align at the top. The pins should project by about ¼–¾in (0.5–2cm) below the card. With the pins in the grooves, glue the second piece of card over

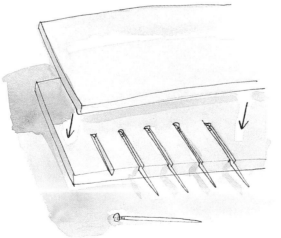

the first, and place the resulting sandwich under a weight to dry.

Experienced marblers, who want to make their patterns as regular as possible, make their combs with lips that rest on the rim of the marbling bath. This ensures an even control of the comb as it is being pulled across the surface of the size.

Mordanting the paper

To prepare the mordant, put 1½oz (42.5g) of alum in a jug and add 1 pint (½ litre) of boiling water. Stir until the crystals have dissolved. (Alternatively, mix the alum into cold water and bring to the boil.) Leave to cool. When the solution is cold, sponge evenly over the paper you want to marble.

(Mark the other side so you know which side has been mordanted.) For best results, marble when the alum has soaked into the paper but the surface is still damp. If you want to prepare the paper at the same time as preparing the size, store all the mordanted sheets flat in a large plastic bag, sealed to make it airtight. Store between two boards with a weight on top. The papers should still be damp enough for use the following day – but don't store them any longer than this, or mould might appear.

PATTERN MAKING

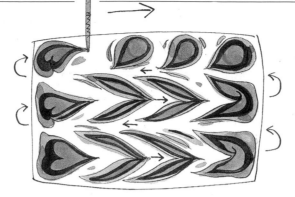

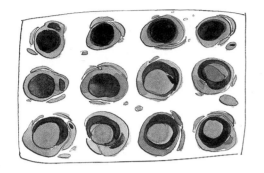

1 *Spread the colours onto the size in an even, overall pattern. Drop the second colour into the middle of the circles made by the first colour, the third into the middle of the circles made by the second, and so on.*

2 *Draw a pointed object (such as a needle or the tip of a paintbrush handle) once through each row of drops of colour. The colours will begin to form a pattern which stays distinct – not spreading slightly as with marbling on other types of size.*

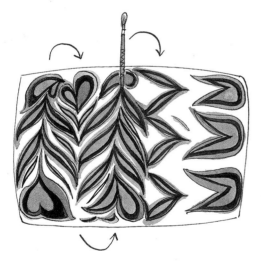

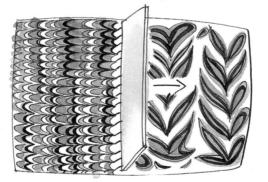

3 *Draw the handle through the colours at right angles to the first movement. The result is a "grid" of flame-like shapes.*

4 *Draw the comb across the size at a slight angle to the surface. Try not to let the teeth penetrate too deeply into the size – they should just skim the surface. Keep your movements slow and smooth: if you agitate the size you will disturb the colours.*

Variations

To vary the patterns, you can move the comb through the colours in different directions, or try zigzag or circular movements. Or you can use a comb in which the pins are differently spaced. Other ways to change the pattern are listed below. Colours treated by methods 1, 2 and 3 should be added last to a bath of size in which other "straight" colours have already been floated, and perhaps already patterned.

a Add very small quantities of oil (olive or cooking) to the colours before you apply them; but only use one drop per colour, and be sure to mix well.

b After making a pattern, take a drop brush charged with oil and shake lots of small drops over the size, leaving them untouched where they fall. This creates interesting pebble-like formations.

c In the same way, sprinkle undiluted white spirit over a simple combed pattern to create an unusual effect with lines and spots of colour.

d Sprinkle a mixture of ox-gall and distilled water (equal quantities or up to 1:10) over a marbled pattern, the colours on the size will move and separate, creating open and veined areas.

e Sprinkle the pattern with a little of the alum solution left over from mordanting.

Right: An example of combed marbling using three different marbling inks on caragheen moss size. White paper showing through is an integral part of the pattern, contrasting effectively with the black.

PAPER IN THREE DIMENSIONS

Although so often thought of as fragile and disposable, paper can in fact be used to create or embellish objects of lasting beauty. Many of these objects, such as the picture frames shown on pages 126–9 and the table top on pages 130–31, have a universal function in the home. Others, such as the jewelry on pages 116–19, are more purely ornamental. However, once you begin experimenting with three-dimensional work and come to see some of its inexhaustible potential, this distinction between the functional and the decorative will probably become irrelevant for you. A cardboard box covered with decorative paper may be valued as much for its appearance as for its usefulness. And a superb piece of marbled paper inside its own complementary paper frame may soon come to seem inevitable and essential when you find an area of wall on which to display it to best advantage.

Of all media, paper is perhaps the one most capable of deceiving the eye. Depending on how it is decorated and the forms into which it is shaped, it can reveal the fascinating intricacy of marquetry, the cool smoothness of ceramics or marble, the graininess of wood. Earrings, brooches and other jewelry in paper can be contrived to look like enamelled metal, as the example opposite shows. This chameleon-like quality, so easily turned to advantage, is one of the great pleasures of working with paper on three-dimensional projects.

Of course, paper is also a time-honoured method of disguise, and this too is an aspect of its appeal. With a covering of paper decorated either commercially or at home, you can quickly transform a tired, battered object, such as an old wooden tray, into something to beautify your home or give away as a special present.

The projects illustrated over the following pages merely hint at the full potential. The only limits are the limits of your own imagination. However, there *are* certain skills to be learned, particularly in the choice and handling of adhesives. Often, very careful measuring is necessary. Learn and practise these skills before attempting anything too ambitious. As you progress, you will inevitably extend your understanding of paper and devise your own ways to achieve the effects you seek.

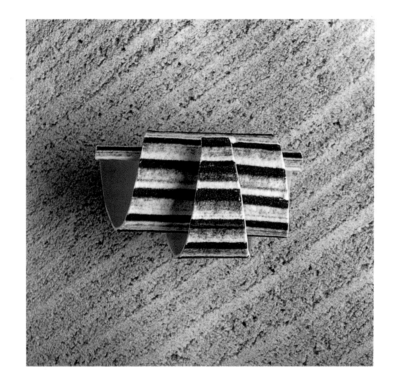

STARTING OFF

To explore the possibilities of paper as a medium for making or covering three-dimensional objects, there are certain basic skills of cutting, gluing and measuring that you will need to acquire. These techniques, which will help you to achieve a professional-looking finish, are all easy to learn. They are simply a matter of patience, precision and an understanding of how paper behaves in different situations.

Some of the projects described over the following pages depend on the use of cardboard for strength and rigidity. Millboard – a high-quality, hard-rolled compact board – is a better choice than bookbinder's chipboard or mounting board, which are rather soft and tend to part. Ticket card, which is lightweight, is useful when you need more flexibility.

When a good thickness is required, you can build up several layers of the thinner grade of millboard (say, 1–1.6mm) by gluing them together – a process known as laminating. The resultant piece is much stronger and more rigid than a single piece of a similar thickness.

When gluing two sheets of card, fit them together and, pressing from the centre, smooth across the surface to chase out any air bubbles. To prevent the boards from sliding as they are pressed, it helps to tape the edges with tiny strips of masking tape, which can be peeled off after drying, taking care not to rip the card surface. Press the boards firmly and allow to dry.

In addition to card, you will need a varied collection of papers of assorted strengths and thicknesses.

It helps to know something about the qualities of different adhesives. PVA (polyvinyl acetate) adhesive, available under various brand-names, gives fast adhesion and is useful for gluing card together. Paste, which wipes off more easily and cleanly than other adhesives, is better for covering card with paper: mix 3 ounces (85g) of plain white flour with 1 pint (0.5l) of cold water and boil as described on page 66. Paste's high moisture content causes the paper fibres to expand when you apply it. As it dries, the paper will shrink slightly, covering the card tightly. Drying takes a while, giving you time to adjust the position of the paper if you wish. Wait for it to dry completely before continuing to work. You can buy a specially formulated paste/PVA mixture: the paste helps to dampen and penetrate the fibres and allows you extended working time, while the PVA adds extra bonding strength and plasticity to the paper.

For covering card with paper, you should generally use paste/PVA mix and applied to the *paper*, which should be allowed to "relax" before you place it on the card. When using PVA adhesive instead, always apply this to the *card*, not the paper. Paste or glue from the centre outwards in a sunburst, as shown in the diagram below (top). This guards against adhesive being pushed under the edges of the sheet. Then, holding the brush upright, stipple all over to ensure even distribution of the adhesive (below right).

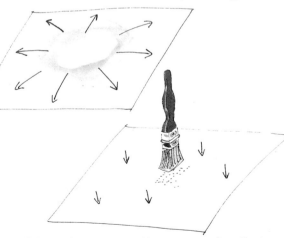

When gluing or pasting, remember that the surface that is being treated will expand to start with and then contract as it dries pulling the other piece into a curve. A very thin paper can warp a thick board considerably. With certain projects, such as the earrings shown on page 116, you can manipulate this tendency to advantage. However, if you want to counteract warpage, you can do so by sticking a third sheet to the reverse of the sheet which is not directly receiving any adhesive. In other words, the aim is to make a sandwich – whether of paper-card-paper or three sheets of paper. For this sandwich technique to be effective, make sure that the two outer pieces are of a similar weight to each other. Remember: the thinner the paper, the more it will stretch and contract.

As far as possible, match the grain directions of the card and paper you are pasting; otherwise, the overall structure is likely to twist.

Paper will be affected by the temperature and humidity of your surroundings. Do not be surprised if it curls and warps in a hot dry room. You can usually persuade it back to its intended form by moving to a damper atmosphere and applying gentle pressure under boards.

When covering an object with paper, there are two methods of joining adjacent pieces to create a continuous surface. You can overlap, or butt-join: both techniques are shown at the top of the next column. The advantage of butt-joining is that you obtain a flat, smooth surface. But because paper swells when wet and shrinks as it dries, you may find a hairline crack occurring between two butt-joined pieces. Straight edges can be butt-joined easily, but curved shapes prove more complicated and are best overlapped. On a flat surface such as a tray, the ridges left by an overlapping join will be more susceptible to wear and tear than the interlocking edges of a successful butt-join.

If you are joining two pieces of paper, or gluing together two ends of the same piece, you will not want excess glue to seep out onto your project when the glued pieces are pressed together. To prevent this, it's a good

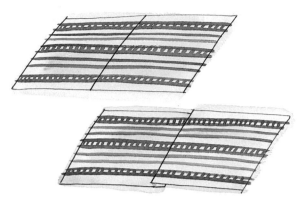

idea to make a simple shield, as diagrammed below. Simply take a sheet of waste paper and fold it in half – diagonally to avoid cockling. Mark the edge of the area you want to paste with a series of pinpricks. Place the folded edge adjacent to the area to be glued, aligning it along the pinpricks. Then apply the paste, drawing your brush in a series of movements in one direction, sweeping over the shield and onto the area to be pasted, as shown below.

To clean up any spills of adhesive, keep by you plenty of damp cotton wool or rag and waste paper (preferably white and un-printed). When pressing a piece of work to

ensure even adhesion, weights may be used. Remember to put water-resistant sheets between the paper and pressing boards. Instead of weights, you could use C clamps to hold the boards together; if so, use thick card to protect the boards from pressure marks.

Cutting

An ability to cut paper properly, as described on page 49, is essential when working on three-dimensional projects. You must take especial care when forming 90° angles, which need to be clean and accurate. Always use a steel edge or set square as a guide, and work on a cutting mat. Keep the blade perpendicular to the paper surface and at an angle which will give a smooth, easy cut. Do not try to cut through thick card in one go: two or three consistent strokes with a firm but unforced pressure will penetrate more easily.

Finishes

Although many articles made or covered with paper look best with their original matt surface, others may benefit from a translucent finish for shine and protection. Finishing in this way is especially appropriate for functional objects which may have to withstand considerable wear and tear. There are various commercial varnishes you can use – for example, microcrystalline wax, polyurethane varnish, and a special varnish made to protect watercolours. However, many of these finishes may be too shiny or obtrusive. To avoid this, you may find it more effective to use PVA adhesive thinned with water to a milky consistency; apply with a brush, allowing several hours' drying time between coats if more than one is required. Finish with a final coat of wax polish if the object is to be handled.

The question of aesthetics

Success when working with three-dimensional objects depends not only on technique but also on artistic judgment. Many beginners tend to err on the side of the over-fussy. If the paper itself has a complicated pattern, the object you make or cover should have a classic simplicity. When juxtaposing different papers, choose them with care. Richly patterned papers could be sepa-rated by plain strips or complemented by larger areas of plain paper so that the overall pattern does not become too much of a jumble.

Many beginners are daunted by "design". Just think of this as a process of selection, and it may become easier. It is worth looking at examples of good design in any area, graphic or three-dimensional. Keep the shapes and ideas simple. Proportion and balance should always be considered – not only in the overall dimensions but also when attaching items such as handles for a box, or ties for a folder.

Choose papers that will complement each other in colour and texture, or else create a deliberate contrast. Just a small area of contrasting colour, such as a handle, or the thumb crescents of a box lid, can look very striking.

Checklist of useful equipment:
Strong blade and scalpel
Scissors
Steel ruler
Carpenter's square or set square
Cutting mat
Assorted brushes: 1in or ½in household paint brushes, purpose-made glue brushes, small synthetic artists' brushes for small areas
Bone folder
Fine-grade sandpaper
Waxed or silicone resist paper or sheet polythene to prevent excess adhesive from sticking to work during pressing
Pressing boards and weights
Foam plastic sheets or old blankets for pressing textured areas
Copy press or bookbinder's nipping press
C clamps and thick card for protection
Cotton wool and rags
Waste paper – white, unprinted
Various finishes
Various adhesives
Punches and needles

COVERING BOXES

You will need:
Scissors
Scalpel or sharp knife
Cutting mat
Bone folder
Adhesive (paste or paste/PVA mixture)
PVA or similar for finishing (see page 97)

You can make the most mundane object attractive by covering it with paper to give it an original and exciting finish. These pages refer specifically to boxes, but you can adapt the same methods for covering a whole range of other objects – old, battered things in need of a facelift, or things you have made yourself. Traditional techniques in other arts and crafts may offer inspiration: for example, collage or mosaics. Pieces of paper may be juxtaposed on a flat base (as in marquetry) or onlaid to give variations in texture and depth (as in embroidery).

This square gift box has been made of millboard and transformed by a covering of marbled paper, a deep yellow lining and a simple rolled-paper handle on the lid.

Almost any item made of card or wood, both of which are porous, will take paste well. If the wood has dried out, seal it with a paste/PVA mixture before covering – otherwise the parched wood will absorb glue from the paper, resulting in unglued areas and air bubbles. Resist the temptation to cover tins, as these usually contain ferrous metal prone to rust, and there is a risk of staining the paper and rotting its fibres. Plastic is also an unsuitable base, as it defies most adhesives.

When covering a box with paper for the first time, perhaps the most difficult skills are getting the measurements right and cutting accurately and neatly. Success is largely a matter of experience. You should practise the techniques of measuring and cutting described below before you cover your first object: this will obviate the risk of ruining specially bought paper or card.

For boxes as well as other complex three-dimensional objects such as trays, it helps to make a measuring gauge to work out the minimum size of paper you will need. This is really just a flexible ruler improvised out of a long narrow strip of scrap paper. You are likely to need two such gauges – one for the length and one for the width. Fold one of the strips around all the corners, and mark the folds with fine pencil marks or pin pricks, remembering to allow for turn-ins.

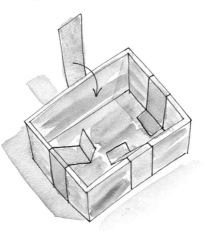

Then repeat for the other dimension. Spread out the strips on the paper you plan to use for covering. You can then see whether it is large enough. If so, lay the box on it using the strips to plot its precise position. Two adjacent edges of the paper should align with the ends of the measuring strips. The other edges of the paper will have to be trimmed as necessary. Transfer the fold or pin marks from the strips to the paper itself.

To paste the paper onto the box use a paste/PVA mixture. You can either paste up the wrong side of the paper; or alternatively, you can dampen the paper with water and apply the paste directly to the faces of the box, one at a time. The latter approach may be more practical for a large surface area, as the paste mix will dry quickly on paper. If following this second method, paste the base, position it correctly on the paper and press down firmly by hand. Turn the whole ensemble over, lay a clean sheet of paper on the top, and firmly smooth down the surface from the centre outwards to chase out air bubbles. Return to the original position.

You can now cut the paper in a cross shape

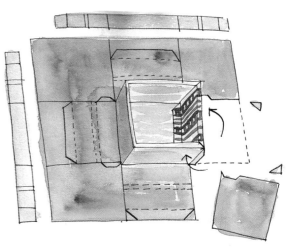

to the measurements marked on the paper. Hold a ruler against the edges and cut with a sharp blade. It is advisable to allow for a small turn-in at corner edges to strengthen them – about ⅛-³⁄₁₆in (3-4mm). For neatness you will often need to mitre the corners (that is, cut them at 45°) where two turn-ins overlap. You can either pre-cut these angles or work each angle with a scalpel as you go along.

After cutting, you can finish the pasting. First paste up the sides where you have allowed for the turn-ins. Draw the paper up, around and down onto each surface, paying particular attention to corners where air is easily trapped and pipes of loose paper form. On the inside, push the paper well into the joins at the corners, or it is likely to pull away on drying. The bone folder is useful for these tasks.

The next stage is covering the inside bottom to hide the edges of the paper already down: see the cross-section, below left.

If you don't have enough of a single type of paper, or want a contrast, you can line the inner surface of the box with different paper. Bring the outer piece over the edge for a ½in (1cm) turn-in (shown above right).

When choosing a box with an overlapping lid (diagrammed below), gauge whether it

will still close properly once the additional layers of paper have been added – remembering that the thickness is even greater on overlapping turn-ins.

To cover the lid, follow the same procedure. If there is a thumb crescent at either side, you can cover these with a small piece of paper before covering the rest. Neatly cut the semi-circle at the edges to form a series of tab-like turn-ins:

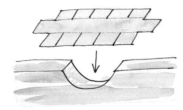

Then sandpaper the turn-ins and cover the rest of the lid leaving just the inside of the crescent showing. Alternatively, cover the lid first, and then add the crescent, leaving the turn-ins deliberately emphasized.

Simple wooden boxes such as cigar boxes are often elegantly proportioned and thus ideally suited to a subdued decorative treatment. If you wish, you can confine the pattern to the lid, as in the marbled example below. The box pictured above shows a more romantic approach, using a pretty plant paper and a decorative clasp. Cigar boxes often have paper hinges, which are lost when you strip off the old covering: if you wish, you can make a note of how the hinge is made and reproduce it in a paper of your choice.

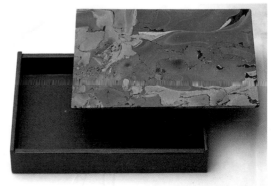

YEOVIL COLLEGE LIBRARY

COVERING GEOMETRIC FORMS

Covered cardboard tubes (such as carpet rolls) can make attractive vase-like ornaments or useful containers, especially for pens, scissors and other desktop items.

A cylindrical container is best covered with a lining of paper to cover the manufacturer's diagonal seams. Any ridges that show should be sanded when dry, before applying the decorative covering. Keep the grain parallel to the length of the cylinder. After you have pasted on the paper (dampen it first if it's especially thick), the turn-in at the open end is easy. Turn the excess ½in (1cm) or so inward over the rim. Mould it flat with a bone folder or nick out a few slim V shapes. For making the base, take the excess paper and mark notches in it; then turn it in and attach a disc of card which has been cut to the circumference of the tube. You may wish to line the inside surface of this disc before gluing it to the cylinder.

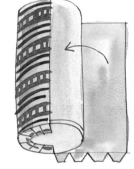

To complete and complement the container, make a simple lid. Glue together several layers of card cut to the outside circumference of the tube and then add several layers cut to fit the inside.

Various objects can be covered with paper to make striking tabletop or mantelpiece ornaments, displayed singly or in pairs or groups. Usually, simple geometric forms are most effective.

Ornamental pyramids are best made from a sheet of cardboard laminated with decorative paper and then folded. First cut the card into a parallelogram shape based on three equilateral triangles as shown here – but without the three flaps. Then paste a sheet of paper onto the card and cut it to the same shape, but this time with flaps added. Making the flaps just of paper, rather than paper plus card, reduces their thickness, giving a neater result.

Pyramids like these can be used as paperweights if filled with some suitable substance such as gravel or dried beans.

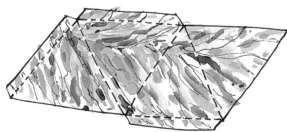

The lid should fit snugly. Remember to allow for the extra thickness of the paper.

As a lifting tab, you can attach a small piece of paper, folded or looped in various ways.

For variation, try making a set of cylinders glued together in a cluster, as shown here. Grouping in this way will confer added strength. If all the cylinders are of the same height, you could easily make a multiple lid out of card. Here, the tubes were first covered with black paper; this was then covered with a paste/PVA mixture and a layer of tissue paper added to produce a delicate crumpled effect.

LAMPSHADES

Paper has been used for making many different styles of lampshade. Now that electric bulbs are available that give out very little heat, the scope for creativity is greater than ever before.

The paper you will need depends on which approach you take. The Japanese, for example traditionally use their fine, tough papers stretched taut on wooden frames, while more usually in the West you will see pleated paper supported by wire frames. However, there is probably more satisfaction to be had in using paper without the addition of an independent framework, relying instead on various methods of giving strength and structure to the paper itself. By varying the paper, you can control the quality of light transmitted. Some white papers will look surprisingly creamy with a light source shining through them. Machine-made papers are good to experiment with, but hand-made papers are preferable for a shade that will look as attractive by day as by night.

You will need:
Paper – white, mostly of cartridge-type thickness (although thinner ones also have their uses)
Ticket card for extra stiffening
Adhesives – PVA, paste/PVA mixture. Use starch paste for laminating thinner Japanese paper
Cutting mat
Craft knife and scalpel
Dividers
Bone folder
Long steel ruler
Scissors – a selection of large, small and embroidery scissors
Unprinted waste paper for cleaning
Punches
Needles in assorted sizes and types
Pressing boards
Foam plastic sheet or old blanket
Waxed paper, silicone release paper or cling film)

Cylinder shades

Cylinder-type shades are strong and easy to make. You can see them singly or in groups, one related to the other, but varying in height and diameter. There are no rules about dimensions, but remember that the larger the shade, the more stiffening you will need to maintain the round shape. Ensure that the grain runs vertically, as this will give added strength. You can make a cylinder shade for a candle or night-light, provided that the naked flame is surrounded by a glass container or jam jar to shield it from draughts.

Work with the paper flat, joining the ends afterwards, once you have glued on the stiffening strips. Try to incorporate the seam or join line into the design where possible.

There are numerous decorative techniques that you can experiment with. For example, crinkle a piece of tissue paper and lay it on a pasted-up sheet of thick paper. Gently push the tissue onto this base with your hand or with a cloth; or use an old pair of nylons, since these have no lint to leave behind. Leave to dry between boards with a resist sheet – wax or silicone paper, or cling film – on top of the tissue and a sheet of foam on top of that to prevent the texture from being flattened completely.

With cylinder shades, it is essential to cut the sides at perfect right angles to the long edges. The laminated paper may be strong enough to stand up on its own; however, if it needs support, cut two strips of thin card about ⅜in (1cm) wide or more, depending on the size of the shade – for a deep one you will need at least ¾in (2cm). The strip at the base might look better if made half as wide again as the top strip. Using PVA, glue the strips to the inside wall about ⅜in (1cm) in from one end and protruding the same amount the other side. In some cases a simple turn-in stuck down on the inside will suffice, as shown in the diagram at the top of the next column.

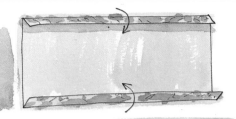

For a neat edge, precrease the folds with a bone folder. Alternatively, stick down additional strips. Overlapping tabs, as shown above and at right, will help to keep base circular.

A pattern of slits, punched holes or geometric cuts in the shade will create intriguing shadow effects.

One approach is to pierce the paper with needles. This kind of pattern looks especially good against a background randomly textured by running a tailor's marking wheel across it in several directions. If you pierce on a soft surface such as a blanket, the burred edges will be more pronounced.

Alternatively, you could make smooth-edged holes with a hole punch. Without the textured edges around the holes, the effect of light coming through is very different.

Although plain cylinders can look effective (far right), simple head and tail borders, stuck in place or woven in, will create decorative interest at the edges as well as added strength. You could also experiment with pierced effects or torn strips of paper on the inside of the cylinder (near left). Crumpled papers will present textural interest.

Decorate a cylinder shade with a pattern of slits by cutting rectangular, angled or curved flaps to let the light shine through.

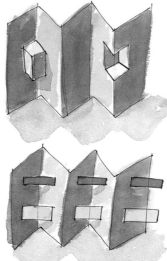

You can also use the slits as a basis for woven patterns (above left). Woven bands of paper will help to hold the cylinder in place.

Folding concertina-wise will give the paper a more rigid structure. Moreover, the width of the folds can be varied to create different levels of shadow. Neat creasing and even spacing are essential for success. Try making a series of slits and weaving bands of paper through, as illustrated above right.

When joining the folds to form a concertina cylinder, tuck the single edge of a fold at one end into the V of a complete fold at the other end. Glue in place with PVA, firmly hold and smooth the two parts until contact is made.

Fan wall lights

The concertina method lends itself to conical shapes, fans or various freestanding forms as well as to cylinders. One of the most attractive types of lampshade is the fan-shaped wall light.

Take a large sheet of paper at least twice as long as it is deep. Mark the centre of a line ½in (1cm) up from the lower long edge. Using dividers pivoted on this centre point, lightly describe a semi-circle and cut around it carefully.

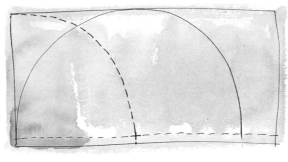

Divide the circumference into even distances and join each of the points to the centre point, using your bone folder to score these lines alternately on either side of the paper. Do one side at a time, remembering to alternate. The extreme tip of the base will need to be cut off to make the folding easier. After making the score marks, fold into a concertina with the bone folder and straight edge. Because you will be folding against the grain, it is particularly important to do this.

The top edge of the fan may be scalloped or shaped, but you may find it better to leave this until the main folding has been done.

The fan will need a support of fishing line threaded through punched or cut holes to prevent the paper structure from sagging. One set of holes should run near the tip of the base, another around the fan's midpoint, as shown in the diagram at the top of the next column.

Before punching the holes, fold the concertina together, making sure that you keep the edges aligned. The faces of the folds may be punched in groups: slip a piece of protective card between each group, and use one punched face as a guide for the next set.

You can also use punched holes for patterning: make a template first as a guide for the design.

The fan will require a shaped back support. Cut a semi-circle from thick ticket card, or card covered with paper. Its width will dictate the final shape of the shade. Punch or pierce holes at the base and sides to coincide with the filament holes in the fan itself, and make a hole for the light source. Glue an inward-turning face at either end of the fan, and attach these faces to the card support, as diagrammed at the top of the next column.

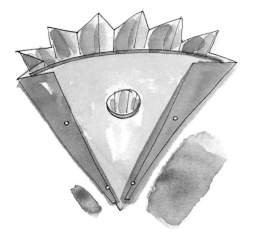

Adjust the threaded filament to give the desired amount of curve to the shade and secure at the back of the support to prevent it from slipping. Tape over the knot with a strip of paper glued in position.

Ordinary bulbs may be used provided that the paper is positioned far enough away from the bulb; but, as a general rule, the new types of miniature fluorescent are safer.

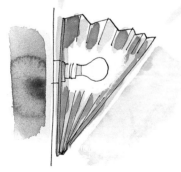

Abstract forms

Lampshades based on sculpted shapes with abstract or geometric forms can become quite complicated. Working with simple ideas will give the most satisfying results initially. You could progress from these to "drawn" shapes based on ornamental or natural forms, all using the same cutting, folding and shaping techniques. Curved forms can be made more rigid by pre-creasing with a bone folder and then semi-folding them:

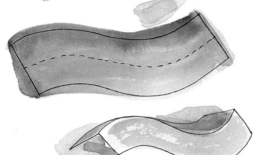

You can achieve a surprisingly three-dimensional effect simply by bending forms you have cut with a blade, backwards or forwards from the main plane of the paper. The light will then shine through the cuts, casting shadows of the projecting shapes. Remember, though, to keep the spacing of the cuts far enough apart to avoid overall weakness or even total collapse of your structure

Delicate scalpel work is necessary to produce silhouetted shapes like this floral bouquet. Cut-outs of this kind may be glued to the inside of a cylinder shade or to a flat screen positioned in front of a light source.

Paper shapes stuck onto translucent paper also offer plenty of scope for silhouetted effects. They can be simple or complicated, free or restrained, using edges that are torn or accurately cut. Depending on the thickness of the cut-outs, they will either keep their secret until the lamp is switched on, or reveal something of their design in subtle shadow even when not lit from behind.

Experiment by tearing strips of a thicker paper, and laying them in place on a pasted sheet of the size you need for a cylinder shade. Paste up a second sheet and lay this over the strips. Press with one side flat on a damp-proof sheet over a board, and cover with another resist sheet and a layer of foam plastic. Lay another board over the top of this. When dry, the side next to the foam will have a slight texture. Keep this to the outside, and join the two ends of the cylinder as before.

BLINDS

Blinds are not only functional but can also be an attractive part of a room's furnishings, blending in discreetly with the decoration or kept tucked away and suddenly revealed as a splash of colour or stunning design.

There are two basic types of blind: the roller blind, operated by a cord and spring action, which causes the blind to wrap around a roller when released; and the concertina blind, which is folded rather than rolled, but again by a cord action. The concertina blind is probably easier to make and more versatile than the roller type, which requires stronger paper.

Concertina blinds
The instructions given below explain how to make a simple concertina decorated by crumpling and dyeing. However, you can experiment freely with other types of decoration – for example, using the paper flat and airbrushing or spattering it, or laminating decorative paper to a stronger plain paper.

You will need:
Strong plain paper – for example, "goatskin parchment" or handmade
White tissue paper – Japanese, or the kind used for model aircraft
PVA adhesive
Paste/PVA mixture
Stiff card – for example, millboard about 1.6–2mm thick – or two wooden battens
Punched hole reinforcement rings
Furnishing or nylon cord
Coloured inks (waterproof or watercolour)
Bone folder
Long straight edge
Dye bath
Shower attachment (optional)
Rubber gloves
Newspapers
Plastic sheeting
Hole punch or drill

Stage 1: measuring and folding
Work out how much strong plain paper you will need, according to the size of your window. Ideally the blind should fit neatly within the window frame, but not too tightly or you will prohibit its movement. Make sure that you have enough paper to form all the folds you require, and to allow for a lightly folded effect even when the blind is drawn down. There are no rules about the width of the folds, but you will probably find it practicable to work to about 1½in (3.5cm). It may be necessary to use several sheets of paper which can be joined after colouring.

Fold the paper concertina fashion, keeping the width of the folds constant for each sheet. Next, open out and crumple the paper. This can be quite hard work, but it is best done not too vigorously or there will be a risk of tearing and splitting.

Stage 2: dyeing
Smooth the paper slightly on a firm surface, using the flat of your hand. It can now be placed in the dye bath. (The larger the dye bath, the easier it is to handle the paper.) A navy-blue cold water dye was used for the example shown on page 108, but you can experiment with a whole range of dyes.

Soak the paper for several hours for a relatively pale shade, or overnight if you want the colour to be stronger. When you are happy with the colour, drain off all the dye solution (which can be kept for dying to a pale colour in the future), then rinse off the excess dye as much as possible with clean cold water; a shower attachment is convenient for this.

At this stage, because the paper fibres will have been weakened during folding, crumpling and dying, breaks may possibly appear in the paper (although this is less likely if it is handmade). These can be mended, however, and incorporated into the general design (stage 4).

Stage 3: drying
Lay the paper on a flat surface on which you have placed plenty of newspaper and then a layer of plastic sheeting. The plastic will prevent the newspaper ink and fibres from sticking to the paper while it is drying.

Stage 4: repairing breaks
When the paper is dry, re-fold it to its original concertina shape. If there are any torn or weak patches, glue pieces of tissue paper over them, on both sides. For extra strength, you may need to add two or three layers of tissue on each side. With a soft paintbrush, paint over the tissue-papered areas in an equivalent or contrasting colour. Once the ink is dry, it is effective to use a fine paintbrush charged with gold, bronze or silver or coloured ink to trace around the patched areas, extending the line to blend with any pronounced creases. This gives you an abstract, cloud-like pattern.

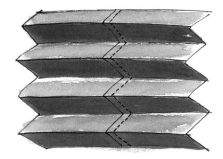

Stage 5: assembly
Join the separate sheets with PVA adhesive or paste/PVA mixture, allowing overlaps of approximately ½-¾ in (1-2cm).

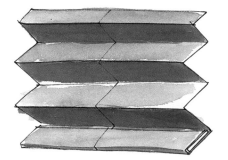

Strengthen the top and bottom edges of the blind with strips of card or wooden battens. If you use card, the grain should run along the length of the strips. Glue each strip in position, tucking it into a fold and covering it completely.

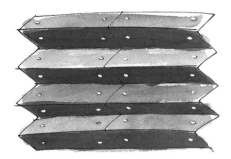

Using a hole punch, make a hole in the same place on each fold, so that a length of cord can be passed through the blind at four points. Reinforce the holes with clear rein-forcements – the kind used for filing.

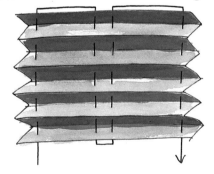

Lastly, compress the concertina blind and thread the cord as shown above. Operating the concertina blind is easy. To open, pull the central loop gently downwards:

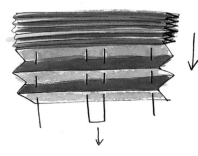

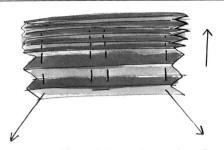

To close, gently pull the side cords sideways and outwards simultaneously, as shown above.

Roller blinds

Roller systems can be bought from fur-nishing stores, and although intended for use with stiffened fabric, they can be used equally well with paper. Make sure that the paper is strong enough to withstand the constant roller action. You can provide added strength by laminating together two or three layers of thinner paper using a paste/PVA mixture.

For a large area you will need to overlap several small sheets. If using machine-made paper, make sure that the grain of all the sheets is running in the same direction as the roller to prevent creasing.

Screens can be opaque or light-transmitting. An opaque screen can be made by applying paper to a solid surface, several panels of which may be hinged together. Alternatively, you could take an old folding screen, give the frame a new coat of paint, and enliven the flat areas of the screen with a collage of decorative papers.

The shapes can be as free as you like, but the grain and stretch of the paper has to be taken into account. Instead of random curved shapes, you might prefer to create the same sense of movement with straight-edged pieces, which are easier to cut and apply.

The techniques for covering opaque screens are similar to those for covering trays and other objects.

Alternatively, you can make a light-transmitting, or translucent, screen – a framework of card or wood with semi-translucent papers stretched across, sprayed with water and allowed to dry to a drum-like tension. Handmade papers worked with embedded fibres are as effective with front lighting as with back lighting.

Japanese-type translucent screens have a serene simplicity. Usually they incorporate plain or self-patterned paper, but there is no reason why you should adhere strictly to tradition. As with light shades, you can create some interesting silhouetted effects by sandwiching cut or torn shapes, threads, fibres or other textured objects into a lamin-ate of two sheets of paper. You then stretch the laminate onto a supporting framework. Such screens can be used over windows or placed freestanding in a room.

Fireplace screens give scope for more three-dimensional effects. Create sculptural interest by folding and cutting techniques, or use a series of simple screens of varying shapes, one behind the other, to give a sense of depth by the play of light and shadow. Of course, paper fire screens are safe only when the fireplace is not in use.

Left: *Concertina blinds will usually need to be made in at least two sections, with an overlapped join, if they are to cover a whole window. On this example, patches of tissue paper were added to cover rips and weak patches made in the paper as it was crumpled, folded and soaked in blue dye. A darker shade of blue was applied to the finished blind with a paint brush, disguising the tissue paper, and finally an outline of gold was added. A blue cord was used to tone in with the scheme.*

Right: *A simple rectilinear wooden grid can be used as a framework for an attractive screen made of individual paper panels. For this oriental-style structure, each of the panels was made up as a "sandwich" of two sheets of handmade paper with lengths of string in between them. After the adhesive between the sheets had dried, some of the lengths of string were torn through the upper layer: these areas of only a single thickness are more translucent than the rest of the screen, and show up paler when lit from behind.*

PAPIER MÂCHÉ

With a minimum of equipment you can make your own bowls, frames and even boxes in papier mâché. The possibilities for shapes are endless, and you can give full rein to your imagination in applying the different patterning techniques you have learned so far. Don't worry if you have never done anything like this before – part of the fun is in discovering the different things you can create, using either of the two simple methods which follow.

You can either use paper in its pulp form or you can paste small, torn scraps of paper over the mould. As you become experienced, you will choose the method that best suits the object you want to make.

Layer method

You will need:
Plenty of strong paper
*PVA adhesive, wallpaper adhesive or starch
    paste*
Selection of household paint brushes
Containers for paste
Shallow dish for paste in use
Newspapers
Bone folder or other flat smooth object
Apron
*Work surface, preferably shiny, or sheet of
    formica or plate glass*
*Football, beach ball or other object suitable
    for use as a mould*
*Assortment of saucepans or similar to hold
    spherical moulds as you work*
*Petroleum jelly or modelmaker's release
    agent*
PVA (diluted) or polyurethane varnish

When choosing your paper, bear in mind that, contrary to popular belief, newspaper does not provide an ideal basis for papier mâché objects, as it is prone to acid attack. However, if you do use newspaper, a heavy coat of paint followed by a layer of polyurethane varnish will help to preserve

and protect the article from the atmosphere.

Any paper that comes into contact with ferrous metal is prone to discoloration. It is therefore best to use paint brushes with plastic, copper or aluminium ferrules.

You can use any type of strong paper, such as computer print-out paper, brown wrapping paper and discarded letters and envelopes. Scraps of coloured paper and colour magazines can be used on the outer layers for decoration.

Any object with smooth sides can be used as a mould for a simple bowl, but one of the easiest to work with is a ball. You can use a saucepan of smaller diameter to provide support for the ball as you work. Onto the rounded surface you build up layers of torn overlapping paper, one on top of the other. A variety of shapes can be made from the same ball simply by varying the area covered. Crisscrossing the grain and overlapping the torn edges will produce a strong laminate which need not be very thick to hold its shape for purely decorative purposes. For a tougher container, however, gradually build up the layers until you feel that the thickness is sufficient. Remember, the larger the bowl, the thicker it will need to be.

Begin with a smaller ball, such as a child's plastic football. Cover just a little more than half the surface with a smooth, thin layer of petroleum jelly or silicone spray to prevent the papier mâché from sticking to its surface. Most balls have a seam halfway across which can be used as a guide when pasting. If this is not clearly visible, emphasize it with a strip of masking tape.

Tear some plain paper into strips and then tear these across into smaller pieces, grading the sizes as you go. You are now ready to apply the paste. If you are using cellulose wallpaper adhesive, mix it beforehand in order to allow time for the grains to swell. Use at the strongest proportions suggested on the packet, diluting if necessary. If you are using a flour paste, mix it to a creamy

consistency – not too thick or it will dry in lumps but not be any stronger.

Place some paste in a shallow dish and brush it on to both sides of the paper pieces – you'll find this process becomes quicker as you get into a rhythm. It's probably not a good idea to soak the pieces, as they pick up too much paste and become difficult to separate.

Starting at the apex, or centre point, of the ball, and working evenly round and down, apply the smaller glued pieces so that they

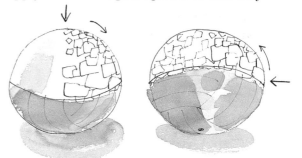

overlap. Gradually increase the size of the pieces towards the mid-point until you overlap the line. For a deeper shape, continue beyond the halfway mark for about an inch (2.5cm), but make sure first that the ball is flexible enough to be easily removed; you can, of course, make the bowl shallower if you wish.

Put on a second layer, overlapping the pieces. This time start at the half-way mark and work upward; then add another two or three layers, working in the same way.

It can be just as effective to decorate the inside of a bowl as the outside, provided that you intend to display the piece at a low level – for example, on a coffee table. This thin papier mâché bowl was decorated in a free pattern of black ink, mottled like an eggshell. First, a fine spatter was applied using a toothbrush dipped in the paint and scraped with the edge of a piece of card, so that colour flew off the bristles. Then larger blobs were flicked on with a household paintbrush dipped in fairly liquid paint.

With a bone folder or smoothing tool, and working firmly from the apex down, push out any air bubbles which may have occurred and squeeze out surplus paste; then put the bowl in a warm place to dry. Once it is dry, you can continue pasting on layers – perhaps five more. For the outer layer you could change to a different colour of paper. Repeat the smoothing process and then allow the bowl to dry out completely – this could take at least two days.

As long as the base (which was the apex to begin with) is worked flat, the bowl should stand firmly enough; and if the laminates are even, there should be an equal distribution of paper pieces all around, making for balance. For greater stability, however, you can work a "foot" by laying a circle of small pieces at the centre of the base, building up with slightly wider pieces, overlapping until a pronounced ridge is formed.

You can thicken and decorate the rim by laying overlapping narrow strips around the edge until you reach the required thickness; then smooth down for a compacted finish.

When the papier mâché is completely dry, gently ease the shape from the mould. It should slide off gradually; it helps to depress the ball to release the vacuum. You will now have a bowl with a smooth inside and a slightly textured outside which you could either leave as it is or decorate it – for example, by painting with watercolour, gouache or acrylic paints, applying the paste and colour method (see page 66), spraying, spattering (page 71) or printing. You could also prepare a marbled surface and gently rotate the bowl along it to pick up the colours.

Once you have decorated the bowl, allow the surfaces to dry, then seal with PVA (mixed to a milky consistency). Polyurethane varnish is also suitable but tends to have a yellow tinge. Or you may prefer to preserve the natural qualities of the matt paper.

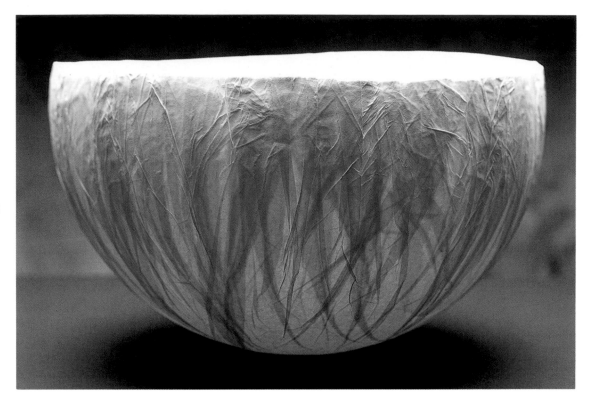

Variations

Thin Japanese papers with long fibres are ideal for making papier mâché objects from moulds that have a finely modelled surface. A surprising amount of detail will be retained, and the overlaps between the torn pieces will tend not to be visible.

As well as using torn scraps, you can make papier mâché-type objects using large sheets of paper pasted well on both sides to relax the fibres, then smoothed gently but firmly over a suitably shaped mould. Build up several layers to give strength.

Even one sheet of paper treated in this way is capable of holding its shape. Strong hand-made paper is the best choice.

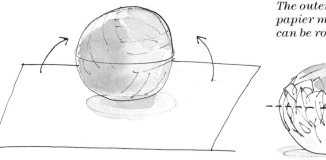

The outer surface of a papier mâché bowl can be roughly tex-tured to contrast with the smooth inner surface. This semi-translucent bowl was built up from ten or so full sheets of very thin paper drawn over a ball and smoothed down. The random overlaps and creases are crucial to the effect.

PULP METHOD

This method of making papier mâché objects is more akin to modelling with clay. You can work with a mould or produce freestanding objects without one, squeezing and shaping the pulp to its required form – a process that is freer and quicker than building up a shape by the strip method. The finer the pulp, the finer the modelling you can achieve. If all you want is a surface for decoration, the pulp can be relatively coarse.

Keep your various colours of paper separate, unless the object is to be given a coloured finish.

You will need:
Waste paper of any kind, except newspaper
Wallpaper adhesive (cellulose or starch), home-made starch paste (85g/3oz plain flour: 0.5 litre/1 pint of water) or wall paper size
Buckets or plastic containers
Large saucepan for boiling the paper
Moulds (optional) – for example, colanders or jelly moulds
Old nylon mesh curtains or large sieve
Cold water dyes or fabric dyes
Rubber gloves
Petroleum jelly or modelmaker's releasing agent
Blunt knives, spoons, pastry cutters, forks or any other kitchen utensils that can be used for patterning and modelling
Blender food processor or mincer

Making the pulp
Tear or shred the waste paper and soften by soaking in hot water, or boiling water for particularly tough papers. Put the mixture through the blender or food processor, mixing plenty of water with each batch, until you achieve the consistency of fine porridge.

Strain the pulp until water ceases to drip; then put it in a bucket or other large container, and mix in wallpaper adhesive or size (prepared according to the instructions

on the packet), or starch paste if you prefer. You should not need to dilute the wallpaper adhesive too much, since there will inevitably be some moisture left in the pulp; on the other hand, it should not be too thick. Stir and squeeze the mixture until it feels malleable. When the pulp has absorbed sufficient cellulose, it should have a *slightly* slippery feeling. Keep aside some of the liquid cellulose or size to brush or spray onto the finished object if it seems to absorb colour too quickly.

Colouring the pulp with dye can produce some interesting effects. Wear rubber gloves for this. Add more or less dye according to the depth of colour required – remembering that the colour lightens on drying. For a mottled effect, combine the dyed pulp with some undyed mixture; work the mixture very gently to avoid spreading the dye too much and creating a "muddy" appearance.

When using a mould, remember to ensure that the piece will not be trapped inside it on completion. An open shape like the one above is ideal.

Remember to smear petroleum jelly over the areas which will be in contact with the pulp. Push the pulp well into the mould, patting it down and pressing it with the back of a spoon to ensure a compacted, even layer. The inside surface of the pulp can be patterned with impressed marks, and the edges or rims pinched or otherwise decorated.

You can make a kind of "box" using the

mould as a "lid" and a matching plate for the base.

Make the "lid" first, dry it and then place in position on the base using cling film or saran wrap between the two pieces, to prevent the "lid" from becoming damp and soggy. When the base dries it will shrink around the "lid" shape and match its edges.

You can form pressed shapes using two identical plates or bowls. Fill one of the pair with pulp until it has an even surface level with the rim. Pat and compress, then set the other plate or bowl on top with weights to press down the pulp.

A scalloped edge can easily be given to a papier mâché bowl or tray by pinching the rim while it is still wet – rather as you might decorate a pastry case.

Whatever kind of mould you use, you should allow a drying period of a few days in a warm airy place. Avoid the temptation to speed up this process, as this may cause the object to distort and the surface of the papier mâché to brown as the sizing agent dries.

If your mould is a deep one, you may have some difficulty in releasing the finished shape. Ease it gradually away from the sides, allowing air to enter between the shape and the mould in order to release the vacuum.

Once the object is thoroughly dry and you have extracted it from the mould, you can decorate it by any of the methods already described for the layer method.

Using pulp without a mould

If you are dispensing with a mould, you should work on a flat surface covered with baking foil that you have greased with petroleum jelly. The foil will help you to release your object after it has dried.

Lay a thick layer of pulp (about 1in/2.5cm) on the foil surface and press firmly to form the outline shape you require. This can be done either with your hands or using any suitable kitchen utensil.

For a mirror or picture frame, find a shape to represent the centre – for example, a saucer – and mould the pulp around it. Then allow the pulp to dry slowly before removing this central template.

Model by layering, with time for partial drying between each layer, rather than trying to manipulate one thick piece. Use a pressing and pinching action to secure the added pieces to the main shape.

Above: *"Braided" decoration and subtle pastel colouring distinguish this matching bowl and mirror frame, made by moulding pulp. To make the mirror frame, the pulp was worked around a circular plate. The "braiding" on both pieces was fashioned with a kitchen knife.*

Right: *If built up thickly, a papier mâché bowl can look as substantial as earthenware. This one has a black finish that evokes a Japanese mood. The mould used was an old colander which left a smooth, almost metallic finish on the outside, with a pattern of round rough patches where the pulp was forced through the holes. The bowl has a satisfying feeling when cupped in both hands. Textures like this can be spoiled by varnishing, leave them unfinished – unless you use a special matt varnish or PVA diluted, which will protect the surface without making it shiny.*

JEWELRY

It is fun to make earrings, brooches, bracelets, necklaces and hairpieces out of paper – perhaps reflecting the contemporary taste for striking contrasts of black and white, or geometric shapes. Being relatively small, paper jewelry will withstand a certain amount of wear. The very lightness of paper ornaments dangled on chains or earring attachments gives them extra animation as the wearer moves around.

Vivid colours and patterns like those shown below are all part of the enjoyment of making paper jewelry. Because the materials are so inexpensive, you can afford to indulge your flamboyant instincts. At the opposite extreme, you can make discreet pieces whose understated elegance belies their humble origins.

You will need:
Adhesive – PVA, starch paste, a PVA/paste mixture or all-purpose adhesive
Firm brushes, including a small one (eg no. 5 watercolour brush) for delicate work. Synthetic fibre is best as it keeps its spring, is longer-lasting than sable and less expensive
Scissors
Cutting mat
Scalpel or sharp modelling knife
Needles (sewing)
Jewelry accessories – for example, necklace threads or cords, earring fittings in silver, silver-gilt or stainless steel, brooch backs, necklace clasps
Knitting needles (various sizes)
Modelmaker's rods or cocktail sticks

Basic techniques

When working with a thin sheet of paper, it is usually best to laminate it to a second sheet for extra thickness. Whichever of the two sheets you paste will expand and contract more than the one applied to it, creating a curve, as shown below:

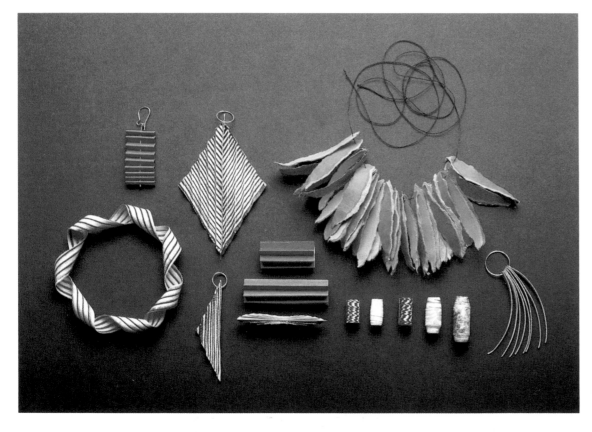

grain

Torn edge pieces have a spontaneous quality and work well with necklaces and earrings in particular. If you want an irregular tear, make it *across* the grain. Tearing *with* the grain is easier and creates a smoother edge.

grain

An effective method is to laminate together two thick sheets in contrasting colours, pasting both sheets, and press flat under a weight to dry. Then tear small elongated shapes to reveal the colour contrast. If you tear by pulling *toward* you, the colour behind will show along the ragged edge. Tearing away from you will make the other colour show on the reverse. You can use both ways to good effect on one piece of paper.

Pierce holes through your shapes with a needle, and thread them onto earrings – or alternatively attach them to earclips with jeweller's adhesive. Several such shapes can be threaded onto coloured beading threads with or without rolled-paper beads between them to act as separators and provide extra weight. You could also suspend pieces from a collar of laminated papers cut from a circle, with a narrow strip taken out of the circle between the circumference and the central neck hole. No fastenings are necessary, as the collar will spring readily back into shape after you have twisted it to put it around your neck.

Curled pieces can have great appeal. This bead and earring were made out of decorated paper laminated together, curled around lengths of dowelling and held in place with a rubber band until the adhesive had dried.

PAPER IN THREE DIMENSIONS **117**

Rolled beads can be used at any scale. For a regular-looking necklace like this one, it's essential to ensure that the pieces of paper for each bead are exactly the same size and cut at the same angle.

Rolled beads

Rolled beads are a classic form of paper jewelry. Cut strips of paper and curl them tightly around a fine knitting needle. Glue the beginning and end of each strip to prevent unwinding. Alternatively, paste the whole length of a strip and tightly roll it around a fine knitting needle that you have waxed or vaselined. You can use one needle for several beads, which you should leave in place until dry.

Elongated triangular strips in contrasting colours laminated together and rolled have considerable decorative potential. For a two-colour effect, cut one triangle slightly slimmer than the other and roll the laminate onto a knitting needle, starting with the wide end. Marbled papers also look good when rolled. All these beads are suitable for threading onto several strands of silk, cotton or wools, depending on the effect you want.

Weaving

By weaving narrow paper strips on a small scale, you can make brooches of all shapes and sizes. Secure the strips with tiny dabs of PVA or appropriate quick-drying paper adhesive. You can glue the completed shape to a plain piece of paper, perhaps of contrasting colour, which will show through the spaces. Onto this backing, which strengthens the decorative lattice, you can glue a brooch attachment.

Instead of weaving narrow strips together like this, you could glue them all in the centre, fanning them out into a starburst of colour.

Concertina folding

You can make concertinas by the simple folding techniques described on page 50, using a bone folder. The narrowness of the folds – anything from 1/16in/2mm to 3/16in/4mm depending on the size of piece required – will help to stiffen the paper. Nevertheless, it is wise to use a stiffish paper

to begin with or to laminate two thin sheets.

Gluing together concertina shapes at right angles to each other will ensure that folds stay closed: use PVA or other quick-drying adhesive.

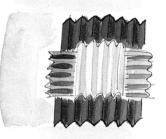

You can also create fan or bow-like shapes by pinching the concertinas at strategic points, and joining with glue, needle and thread or a glued paper band. Bow-shaped concertina hairpieces can be given a sense of movement by dangling twisted paper strips from them.

Fluting (see page 53) requires more patience than folding but achieves a softer effect. To ensure that the corrugations are even, insert knitting needles or modelmakers' rods. For small pieces, cocktail sticks are also useful.

If you wish, you can leave a flat area between each flute for greater adhesion.

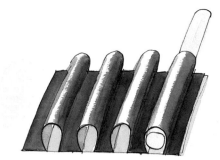

A length of fluting can be curved and formed into cylinders or semi-curved shapes with flat backs for brooch or earring attachments.

Paperchain folding

This method is traditionally used for paper-chain decorations. In miniature, you can apply the same technique to bracelets, necklaces, even earrings. Choose fairly stiff papers. With machine-made paper, ensure the grain lies along the short length.

Take two strips of paper equal in width and length but of contrasting colours. Fold to make a square flap at one end of one of the strips. Paste this flap and press the second strip onto it at right angles to the first. With the first strip uppermost, fold the second strip over – and continue in this way alternately, ensuring that the square is evenly maintained. When the chain is long enough glue the ends together.

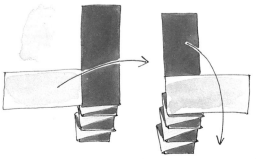

CARDS

There are so many cards available for every conceivable occasion, but they can be expensive and will, after all, be another person's idea. Although they can be attractive, it is sometimes fun, and always more personal, to make your own.

The Victorians made exuberant, fanciful cards and developed techniques to manufacture highly intricate ones whose pierced and pop-up effects make present-day cards look quite simple by comparison, despite the advances of technicolor printing. Some of the ideas of the early card-makers can easily be carried out in today's idioms, with bold colour combinations and simple cutaway shapes. Or, for more subtle cards, you could use the textures and gentle tones of hand-made paper, exploiting the play of light and shade on carefully cut shapes to add a sense of dimension. Architectural forms, with doors and windows, are a useful source of inspiration, lending themselves well to the usual rectangular shape.

You will need:
An assortment of papers and card
Rule or straight edge
Fine pencil
Dividers
Scissors
Sharp knife and scalpel
Adhesives – paste, PVA or mix
Bone folder
Cutting mat
Pressing boards and weights
Waxed or silicone paper
White, unprinted waste paper

If the paper you wish to use is too thin, remember that you can always paste two or more sheets together. Obviously, the size of card you want will affect the choice of thickness – very thick card or paper will be too bulky for a small card which is going to be folded.

The bone folder and rule are essential aids to making sharp folds. Where you have a series of regular shapes, it is important to use a pair of dividers to ensure constant measuring: when marking measurements with a pencil and ruler, there is a greater risk of slight error. Use the grain of the paper to help you: as usual, it should be parallel with the main fold.

The vertical shape with a side is stronger on the whole, and stands better – although you may occasionally wish to make a horizontal shape with a top fold. Follow the basic rules of folding as described on page 50. After pre-creasing with the bone folder and rule, ease the free half up against the edge of the rule and finish by carefully smoothing down that half at the fold – you could do this through a spare sheet of paper to prevent shining or otherwise marking the surface of the finished card.

You can dramatically change the character of the card by varying the position of the fold, or by making more than one fold in the same piece of card: These are just the more obvious possibilities:

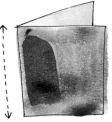 

Cards of this type can be effective if two colours are laminated. It is advisable to dampen both papers before pasting, in order to relax the fibres equally: otherwise, as the pasted sheet contracts on drying, pronounced curving or warpage will occur. Some kind of fastening

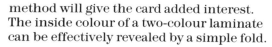

method will give the card added interest. The inside colour of a two-colour laminate can be effectively revealed by a simple fold.

Remember, though, to leave space for your message, without which the card will not be complete. If you laminate a decorated paper with a plain one, try to choose for the plain paper a colour that occurs in the patterned one, as this makes for a more harmonious effect. It makes sense to have the plain colour where the message is to be written.

Folding the paper in half before you begin gives greater strength, and also allows for hidden pop-up shapes.

To discover some of the possibilities, it is helpful to look at childrens' pop-up books with their clever paper engineering; some seem incredibly complicated, but all are based on simple methods. They tend to have added components, but you can achieve a certain amount of movement simply by cutting and folding the single piece of paper you are working with.

It's a good idea to work your pop-up shape out on rough paper, to make sure that it won't protrude beyond the edge of the card. It will generally have to extend from the centre fold to a little less than half way across each face. However, the precise arrangement depends on whether the shape is angled or straight.

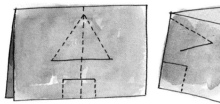

For the tree shape or triangle, shown above, it is best to cut the bottom as a shallow V: this will show as a straight horizontal when the card is opened up.

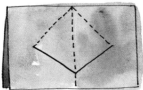

After you have made the cuts, "draw" their folding lines with the bone folder. Then ease the folds backwards or forwards with your fingers to make the shape stand out when the card has been folded again to its original, closed state.

Origami folding can be a source of ideas to adapt for card-making, and it is worth looking at some of the books available on the subject. The paper you use should generally be fairly thin to allow for multiple folding, but if the number of folds is limited you have more choice of textures and thicknesses.

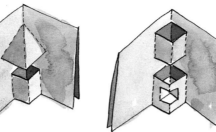

Papercut cards
You can create a whole range of versatile and surprising effects by cutting through the paper of a folded card to make various kinds of pattern. Practise with simple, cleanly cut shapes before venturing on to more complex

designs – it takes a little time to become familiar with the kinds of shapes and lines that you can cut easily with a knife. Curves are difficult, and although there are swivel knives which will make them easier to cut, there is still no really effective free-wheeling blade on the market. However, in some countries, especially China, there has been a tradition of the most remarkably controlled and intricate paper cutting. The paper is very fine, which allows for a lightness of touch and less "drag" than occurs with thicker papers. When attempting your papercuts, you must be prepared to adapt the shapes and techniques to the kind of paper you are using and the overall effect required.

Apart from single shapes cut into the paper, try cutting or piercing decorative borders or creating an overall pattern that dominates the front of the card. As with cutting stencils, you must ensure that the cuts are not too close, and that there are large areas of uncut paper between areas of

pattern to hold the card together firmly. Woven effects, like those shown below, are an interesting avenue of exploration.

You can make a more complex card using three laminations – two thicker papers and one tissue-thin. Cut a simple window out of the front layer of the card, paste the edge of a piece of Japanese tissue cut to size and stick it in position on the inside edge of the window. After pressing the tissue in place, mask the card frame and spray the tissue finely with water. This will relax the fibres, which will tighten on drying to a drum-like skin. When the tissue is dry, paste up the back layer of card, which should have a matching window cut in it, and press onto the first card, sandwiching the tissue. Press between blotting paper or clean resist paper.

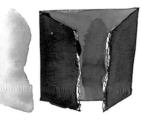

A variation on this method is to imprison shapes of paper between two layers of tissue framed in the same way. This will create a silhouette effect, like shadow puppets.

Torn edges can be used to create a good contrast with clean-cut shapes. Making tears in a two-colour laminate (as described on page 117) is especially effective.

GIFT BAGS AND WALLETS

You will need:
Card, no thicker than 1/16in (1.6mm)
Decorative paper
Waste paper or waterproof paper
Paste/PVA mixture
Brush for applying adhesive
Bone folder
Hole punch
Ribbons, coloured cord or thread

You can make attractive bags and gift wallets using paper, card or card covered with decorative paper you have made or bought. To make a simple gift bag prepare a cross-shaped sheet of paper, as in the diagram below, having first marked out the dimensions on a rough sheet. For a large bag you may need to join three pieces of paper – adding side panels to the long central strip from which the base and sides are formed. Add about 1in (2cm) for the turn-ins on the flaps.

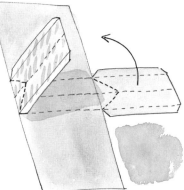

Fold through the centre to give a T shape, keeping the decorated sides of the paper on the inside. Open the sheet out and with the decorated side face down, fold the uncreased side flaps into the centre and open them out again. Next take the other two flaps (those with the turn-ins), fold them into the centre and open out again. Then fold one corner of one of the flaps outwards back on itself at a 45° angle to the long edge of the bag. Open out and repeat for the other corner. You

should now have a triangle creased on the flap, as shown above. Repeat for the second flap. Open the paper out again and bring the flaps up by pushing them in at the pre-creased triangles, pushing the centre fold in from underneath at the same time.

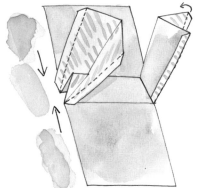

Paste up the turn-ins on the flaps, with a sheet of waste or waterproof paper behind the turn-ins to protect the rest of the bag. Bring the sides up and press together firmly, making sure that the edges are neatly aligned. Repeat this process for the second side.

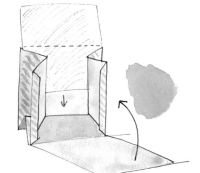

To close the bag you could fold the top over and secure it with a paper clip but for a more secure and professional finish, reinforce the top of the bag by gluing a strip of thin card just below the edge of the paper which can then be turned over to conceal it. Next make holes with a hole punch, thread ribbon or cord through and tie in a bow.

As an alternative to the gift bag you could make a wallet from card covered with paper. You will need three pieces of covered card – one for the base and flaps and the other two for the concertina sides.

Make the base and flaps first: take a single piece of covered card of the size you want your bag to be, and fold the ends in to meet in the middle, using a bone folder to make a neat crease. Open the sheet out and fold the ends in again, this time about 1¼in (3cm) short of the first creases. This will give you the folds for the base and flap. For the sides, take two pieces of card the same width as the larger sheet but one third of the length. Fold each piece widthways from one end to the other, concertina fashion, each fold about 1in (2cm) wide. (Or make fan-shaped pieces as for the wall lights described on p 104.) Keeping the concertina compressed, lightly glue one side and position it as shown below. Repeat for the   second concertina.

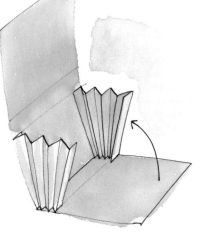

Paste up the second side of the concertina and bring the front flap up to meet it, pressing firmly and making sure that the edges are neatly aligned. Fold the other end of the sheet according to the pre-creased lines so that it comes down over the front of the wallet.

Clutch bags, gift bags or "wallets" can be made in a variety of styles, with flat, creased or concertina sides. It is impossible to be too dogmatic about uses and methods of construction, as these will vary according to personal taste. To finish off your project, you can sew or glue on "buttons" of laminated paper and fasten them together with thick thread in a figure-of-eight loop, as in the example in the foreground of this picture. The flap (if any) may be straight, V-shaped or diagonally angled, and may contrast with the rest of the bag or match it exactly.

123

COVERING TRAYS

You will need:
Scalpel
Cutting mat
Bone folder
Steel ruler
Marbled or other decorative papers
PVA adhesive and paste/PVA mixture

Over the years, trays that are in regular use tend to chip, crack or otherwise become shabby. By giving an old tray a covering of decorative paper, or a mosaic of different papers, you can transform it into an object to treasure.

In covering a tray with a deep inside edge, as in the photograph opposite, there are two stages – first the frame, then the base.

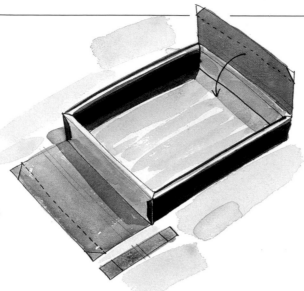

To cover the frame you will need four strips of paper – one for each side. Each strip is laid just over the inside join of frame and base, forming a narrow lip on the base and running over the inside and outside edges of the frame and round onto the underside of the base, where you should allow a turnover of around one inch (2.5cm). Use measuring strips as described on page 98 to determine the dimensions of the paper you will need. For the length allow about ¼ inch (5mm) extra at each end for turn-ins at the corners. These will strengthen vulnerable points.

To soften and relax the paper, dampen it before pasting. The grain of the paper should run lengthways.

Apply the longer sides first. For a smooth finish, sand down the little corner turn-ins at the outer edges; you will hardly notice them when the shorter sides are pasted down over the top – this time to the edges of the corners.

It is best to work the inside angles of each corner as you go along, rather than pre-cut each strip: they may vary slightly, and the paper may move as you work it.

The corners must then be mitred. Bring over the turn-ins and, holding the scalpel at a 45°

angle, cut through the overlapped strips. Remove the underpiece, and smooth down the two strips to make an even surface.

You are now ready to cover the tray's base. Start from the frame and work inwards. The best way to work out the pattern is to draw the rectangle of the tray in proportion as a basis for doodling: you can scale down the size by drawing a diagonal, as shown in the first diagram below. The other three diagrams show some basic pattern ideas for a mosaic. The variety of papers will create sufficient interest even in a very simple pattern.

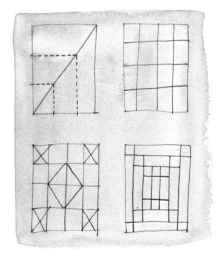

A mosaic covering such as the one illustrated here requires careful measuring. When you have decided on the design, measure the base and divide up the result mathematically to give you the dimensions of each unit of pattern. Or alternatively, if you suffer from a mental block about numbers, cut pieces of scrap paper the length and width of the tray's base and fold them several times to create a template for measuring the pieces that will make up your pattern. Cut any long strips along the grain – even if they are planned to criss-cross – to avoid the risk of stretching.

FRAMES

It is always satisfying to make frames for your own pictures. Obviously, frames made out of card and paper won't support the weight of an oil painting. However, prints, watercolours, photographs, embroidery samplers or any other lightweight objects – even small mirrors – pose no problems.

Almost any kind of paper is suitable, but you should use strong paper for the outer frame edges. Good-quality machine-made papers are perfectly acceptable if you respect the grain direction.

You will need:
Card or board – preferably millboard
Adhesives – quick-drying PVA or paste/PVA
   mixture for structural parts; paste or
   paste/PVA mixture for covering card
Brushes of various sizes for pasting. Use
   synthetic artists' brushes for small areas
Cotton-wool or cotton rag
Strong cutting blade and holder (for card)
Scalpel or fine blade for delicate cutting
Cutting mat
Waxed or silicone-resist paper, or sheet
   polythene to prevent excess adhesive
   from sticking work to surface during
   pressing
Pressing boards and weights
Bookbinders' nipping press or copy press if
   available
C-clamps to use with pressing boards as an
   improvised press – remember to protect
   work with thick pieces of card
Fine-grade sandpaper
Bone folder
Fine pencil
Carpenter's or engineer's dividers
Masking tape
Sheets of foam plastic – useful for pressing
   raised surfaces

Although these paper frames have moulded profiles (described in more detail on page 129), they rely mainly on variations in tone, pattern and texture.

The object to be framed should be your starting point: it's usually less satisfactory to make a frame first, and then look for something to put in it.

A simple card frame has three main components: the backing, the window mount and the strips of card and/or paper that make up the "mouldings". When framing a deep object such as a mirror, you will need to build laminated strips all around as a base for the window mount.

Before you begin, consider carefully the proportions of the mount itself, and its dimensions in relation to the picture. The depth of the mount at the top is usually equal to the width of the mount at the sides, but the depth at the bottom is greater in order to avoid the impression that the picture is sliding down. This principle can be applied to other items in this section: handles, ties and trimmings will usually be placed nearer the top than the bottom of the article in order to achieve a sense of balance.

Cut strips for the mouldings. The strips of card and/or paper that make up the "mouldings" of the frame should have the grain running lengthways. This helps to strengthen the structure and prevents the support boards from warping. Had the grain been running across the short width, the narrow strips would tend to be flexible and bow. Card in narrow widths becomes rigid because it is more difficult for it to warp across small dimensions.

Remember the need to cut very precise right angles, and help yourself by using a carpenter's square and a heavy steel ruler. Glue up the backing boards using PVA. Fit them together, pressing from the centre outwards to prevent air bubbles. To prevent them from slipping during pressing, tape the edges with tiny strips of masking tape which can be peeled off easily afterwards.

Cut strips for the outside edges of the frame. Those at top and bottom should be the full width of the boards; those at the sides should be the length of the boards minus two strip widths.

It is best not to mitre the corners, as this makes them vulnerable. You can strengthen them by alternating the second layer – that is, making the *side* strips the full length of the boards.

Cover the window mount with a whole sheet of decorative paper. Allow between ½–1in (1.2–2.5cm) turn-in width all the way round. Apply paste or paste/PVA, to the paper then lay it carefully on the window mount board and smooth out air bubbles before pressing. Prepare corners of turn-in, paste and turn over, then working from the

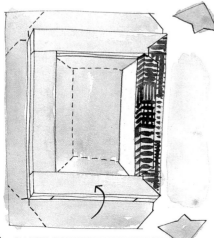

back on a cutting mat, trim inside the picture rectangle leaving a ½in/1cm turn-in. Mitre the corners before gluing onto the back of the mount.

If your design allows areas of the backing board to show, these too need to be covered with paper. Allow to dry under pressure, or the paper will pull the boards into a curve. To prevent warpage, paste another sheet onto the back to counteract the pull, matching the grain directions.

The moulding strips can be covered in paper independently and glued in layers, creating a stepped effect. Cut the paper to size allowing for a turn-in of ½in/1cm or more, and paste it with a paste/PVA mixture. Place the card in the centre, smooth it down and cut the corners to give a 45° mitre. Use a bone folder to ease under each paper edge, fold it up at right angles to the card, and smooth down the turn-in.

If you intend to glaze the picture, take this into account when planning the moulding; you must leave a space between glass and picture to prevent the picture from going mouldy.

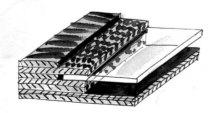

On the topmost moulding strips, you might consider a turn-in wide enough to wrap round the frame edges onto the backing board. This will neaten and strengthen the layered edge.

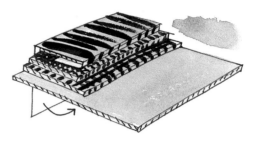

When pressing together the laminated layers of the assembled frame, place a sheet of plastic foam on top, with a pressing board over it. This foam is also useful for pressing together surfaces which have been contoured by the addition of mouldings.

To create an embossed effect with raised surfaces, glue pieces of thin card or thick paper to the card you are using for the frame. Then cover with paper and press under foam. It is surprising how clearly the dampened paper will reveal the outline of the underlying card or paper.

After assembling the main boards and mouldings, you can add smaller elements such as paper-covered squares, triangles, mosaics and so on.

The mount may be joined to the frame with a paper hinge, or glued in place for permanent framing. You can also use a hinge to fix the picture in place. Use paste, as this allows you to remove the image by dampening if required.

When attaching eyelets, hooks or rings to card-and-paper frames, insert the screws at the thickest parts. Card fibres do not grip as firmly as wood. It may be necessary to reinforce the attachment with PVA or multi-purpose adhesive.

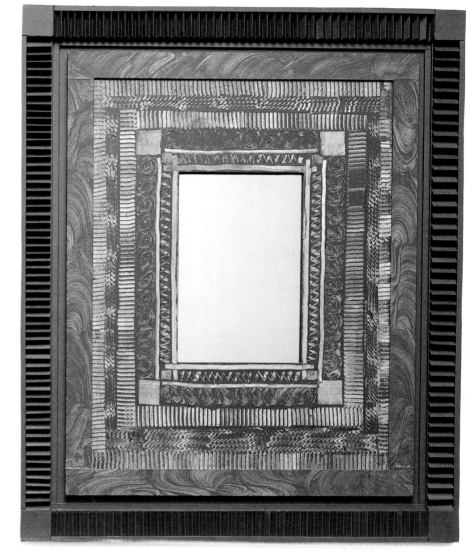

When the colour scheme of a frame is simple and austere, you can afford to make the structure and pattern relatively elaborate. Both frames here display a wide range of techniques. The papers used for the mounts have been decorated by the paste and colour method (see pages 66–69). Left: A triangular pediment flanked by pointed "finials" gives an architectural appearance to this design. The frame includes strips of torn black paper overlapped in a wavy pattern: these appear not only on the top panel, above the pediment, but also on an inner moulding. Separating this moulding from the outer frame is a strip of coiled paper. Notice how squares of different sizes in the corners are echoed in the paste-colour pattern. Right: Narrow strips of paper or thin card folded concertina-wise are an attractive detail to incorporate into a frame. Contrasting with the folded border, there is an inner moulding built up in layers of cardboard and covered with black paper decorated with swirls by the paste-colour technique.

TABLE TOPS

A recessed table top which would normally be covered with ceramic tiles could instead be used as a base for card tiles covered with decorative papers. To make the most of this approach, combine a variety of tones, textures and patterns. Papers handmade from rag linen, cotton linters or plant materials will have a subtle effect and can be further patterned by techniques such as creasing, fluting and punching. Plain machine-made papers offer scope for more colourful decoration – for example, by the paste and colour method or by spattering (see pages 66–69, 70–71). For a more tile-like finish around the edges of each square, turn the paper over onto the back, as shown below – but only if the paper is thin enough to bend easily.

Non-reflective glass, although more expensive, is preferable; ordinary plate glass reflects light and has a greenish cast which can detract from the subtleties of the paper. For maximum versatility, glue the tiles and edging to a sheet of card cut to fit the recess in the table; this way, you can easily remove the decorative insert and replace it with an alternative.

Paper tiles need not be vividly coloured to make an attractive pattern. In this example, the tiles show a subtle range of tones, from pale cream to dark buff. Shadows define the patterns. Notice how the natural colours complement the pale wood frame. The squares use the whole vocabulary of techniques for manipulating paper, including tearing, crumpling, piercing, folding, slitting, weaving and impressing. Note especially the contrast of roughly torn and precisely cut or folded edges.

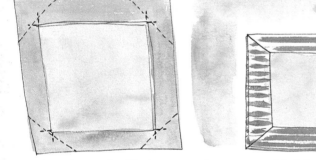

Once the tile is covered, you can add strips of torn paper for a decorative effect:

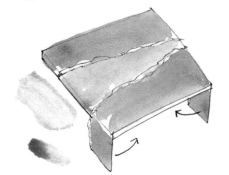

The table or border must be made in such a way that the glass is raised slightly above the tiles to avoid crushing them.

Tabletops could also be made with a deep boxlike space beneath the glass, containing three-dimensional tiles of various thicknesses. These could be covered with decorative paper, just like boxes (see pages 98–99), and arranged in patterns to show the sides as well as the tops – rather like a model of a city or complex architectural model of a building.

Other variations could be made using hexagonal or octagonal shapes of table. The tiles could then be diamonds and triangles.

Another idea is to use an edging decorated, say, by the paste-colour method (see pages 66–69) surrounding one large square decorated by the same technique. Experiment with contrasting textures and patterns.

DESKTOP PROJECTS

Desks all too often bring out in us a propensity for clutter. We tend to buy items such as notebooks, pencils, pencil holders and blotters in a wide range of discordant styles, without any regard for their compatibility. To create a more organized impression, you can buy desk equipment that is unified by a particular decorative theme. For example, these products from Il Papiro, despite their colour differences, are co-ordinated by their marbled paper coverings, in an historic style characterized by overlapping "peacock's-tail" shapes.

If you prefer to attempt such things for yourself, perhaps using papers you have decorated, it takes a little time to master the techniques. The first stage when cutting pencils is to make a template — a rectangle of paper that will roll around the pencil leaving a slight overlap. Once you have trimmed this to the correct width, you can use it as a guide for cutting the paper you intend to use on the pencils. Paste up each covering and place the pencil along one edge; then, in a simple, firm, continuous movement, roll the pencil and paper together until the two edges meet.

The procedure for covering boxes is described on pages 98–9. Folders, suitable for holding letters, documents or anything else you need to keep flat, can be made in a number of ways; some suggestions are given on pages 134–5. Ties on three sides and a half-binding (that is, a strip of contrasting paper along the spine and triangles on the outside corners, as shown below) add a pleasing sense of tradition. It takes only a little ingenuity to extend these approaches to other desktop projects, such as blotters and envelope holders.

Marbled papers have a traditional association with bookbinding: they have been used for centuries to make patterned endpapers. It is perhaps for this reason that marbling seems so appropriate for desktop projects intended for use in the study, such as the folders, boxes and other items illustrated on these two pages.

FOLDERS

You will need:

Paper of any kind, perhaps decorated by
  method described on pages 62–93
Cardboard of about 1/16in (1–1.5mm)
  thickness – for example, millboard or
  other bookbinder's board
Ribbons
PVA
Paste/PVA mixture
Brushes for applyng adhesive
Strong knife for cutting card
Scalpel
Scissors
Straight edge
Set square or carpenter's square
Cutting mat
Wax paper or polythene sheet
Pressing boards and weights

It is relatively easy to make a decorative folder for stationery, letters or documents, but you must take care to avoid warping: the whole point of a folder is that it keeps things flat. For neat results, follow the usual guidelines on grain direction, choice of adhesive and pasting techniques.

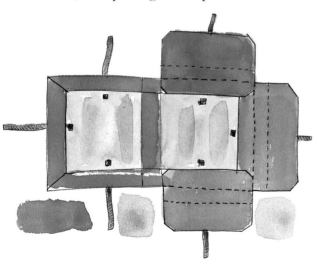

The first step in making the simple folder

shown in the previous column is to cut two boards to the required size, using a set square or carpenter's square to make perfect right angles. Then cut the cover paper to size, allowing at least 5/8–1in (1.5–2cm) for a turn-in on each of the four sides and a generous centre width which will become the spine. Place the boards in position on the underside of the covering paper, and mark their corners with pin pricks using your dividers. You will later mitre the corners of the covering paper, leaving a space at the corner 1½× the thickness of the board, to make turn-ins as shown below: this ensures that the corners are well covered.

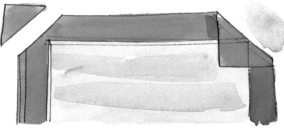

Before this, however, you should apply the adhesive. Paste up the first board and place it on the location marks you have made. Then press down firmly, turn over and smooth your hand all over the surface of the paper to ensure even sticking. It's best to do this with a clean sheet of waste paper on top to prevent marking the decorative surface. Repeat this procedure for the second board. Holding a rule against the top edge of the first board, as shown below, helps you to get the positioning exact:

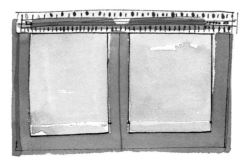

Simply place the second board up to the rule and against the spine mark and press down under a weight after smoothing.

After the adhesive has dried, prepare the mitred corners as shown in the centre diagram on this page. Paste and fold down the turn-ins on all four sides. Run your bone folder against the edges of the boards at the spine for a neat finish and to ensure adhesion of the turn-in at head and tail.

An inside lining of contrasting paper looks effective, but before applying this you should make and paste down the flaps. These may be either of strong paper or of paper-covered card. With the latter method, care is needed when covering the angled corners. Whichever method you are using, make sure that the grain direction runs the length of each flap to ensure neat, flexible folds. The basic stages of the procedure are shown below:

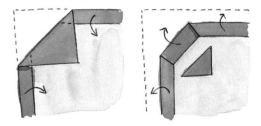

First, fold in the corner of the covering paper to make a triangular turn-in. Then turn over the side turn-ins of the covering paper. Cut off the tip of the triangle so that the edges of the three turn-ins line up with each other. Then spread the paper out again to its original form by folding back the side and corner turn-ins.

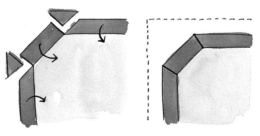

At each side of the angled turn-ins, your fold marks will have formed two little triangles. Cut these out, as shown at the foot of the previous column. When folded down again, the edges of the three turn-ins should overlap slightly: these overlaps are necessary since when the paper dries it may contract and leave a gap.

After covering each of the flaps, paste them in position on the folder. Add the ribbon ties, thread them through pre-cut slits in the covers and glue down on the inside.

The ties will be hidden on the inside by the lining paper. Cut this as a single sheet covering boards and spine, and overlapping the turn-ins of the outer cover to leave a border of about ⅛in (2−3mm) on each side. Or you can run a strip of patterned paper down the inside spine, then add the lining paper as two sheets, with a space between showing the pattern. For extra strength you can use a spine stiffener between the two boards with a ³⁄₁₆in (4mm) gap either side.Glue down the turn-ins on the spine strip at head and tail, and line as before.

To prevent smaller documents from slipping out, you can add a rigid triangular pocket of paper-covered cardboard, as shown below. You need a piece of card cut to a triangle, as well as two narrow strips for the sides. Assemble the sides and covers with a single sheet of paper, leaving two paper flaps by which to attach the pocket to the lining of the folder. The long side of the triangle will have a turn-in at the edge and the underside should be lined to counteract warpage.

Flaps are a practicable alternative to an interior pocket. The grain should always run lengthways on each flap. In this example, a fore-edge flap with a straight edge hides the angled corners of the flaps at head and tail. The basic construction is shown in the diagram (right). Simple black ribbons have been run through slits in the cover and anchored on the inside with PVA, before attachment of the inner lining.

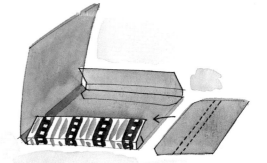

Sheets of paper that have been strikingly decorated need only a plain card surround to show them off to best advantage. These examples owe their impact to a bold colour that has been subtly graduated in intensity. For the piece at far left (above the fire extinguisher) the paper was crumpled into a ball, lightly spread out again and sprayed with colour at an angle, using an airbrush. After the paint had dried, the sheet was smoothed down a little more – but again without flattening – before being mounted on plain white card. The other examples depend on geometrically folded areas, contrasting with random crumpling. These four panels together make up a deliberate progression, with zigzag folds involving more and more of the paper area.

MAKING BOOKS

Bookbinding is a craft older than printing. Beyond its functional purpose to preserve important information, it has the capacity to lend beauty and dignity to the pages held within decorated or plain covers.

The techniques involved in making up, covering and decorating a book are infinite, but you can tackle the simpler methods using a minimum of readily available equipment, even if you have never done any bookbinding before.

It is a good idea to start with the most basic form which comprises just one section of paper and for which only a simple, soft cover and the minimum of sewing are required. You could then progress to the multi-section or "papillon" book where a more complicated sewing technique is needed to hold the sections together and attach them to the cover. Alternatively, you could attempt the surprisingly simple, unsewn concertina-style book made from one very long sheet of paper, or from several sheets joined together.

Instructions are also given in the following section for Japanese-style books, where single rather than folded sheets are sewn with the cover. A more chunky version of this type of book can be made into an album,

using heavier paper and adding extra strips between each sheet at the spine to accommodate photographs, theatre programmes or other memorabilia you may wish to preserve.

Once you have mastered the sewing methods needed to make books with soft covers, you can go on to make hardcover books. These are much easier to make than you might expect, as the covering principles are similar to those used for covering boxes (described on pages 98-9). Hardcovers are excellent vehicles for the decorative papers you have either made or bought.

This chapter shows you how to make a whole range of different books with both soft and hard covers, but does not attempt the more complex methods used by professional bookbinders to bind very thick volumes. These require a great deal of skill and perhaps a longer familiarity with bookbinding, but once you have mastered the basic procedures, it is well worth bearing in mind that there are whole books devoted to the craft of bookbinding and these will help you develop and extend the skills to which you will be introduced in the following pages.

SIMPLE BOOKS

The following list of equipment and materials applies to any of the methods described in the following pages for making books with soft covers. Additional items which you will need if going on to make hard-cover books are given at the end of the list.

You will need:
Paper of any kind, but not too thick to start with. For different effects, experiment with machine-made, mould-made, handmade or Japanese papers
Strong knife for cutting card; scalpel
Straight edge Scissors
Cutting mat or surface
Needle with short eye, but large enough for the thread you are using; special bookbinders' needles are available
Thread – linen is preferable to dressmakers' which is too fine and may cut the paper
Dividers
Set square or carpenter's square
Wax paper or polythene sheeting to prevent damp from the glued covers permeating the pages of the book
Pressing boards
Waste paper
PVA; paste/PVA mixture
Brushes for applying adhesive. A flat artists' brush or synthetic watercolour brush is useful for small areas
Three-dimensional objects suitable for impressing and embossing, for example, string, cut-out letters and leaves
Bradawl
Card of about ¹⁄₁₆in (1–1.5mm) thickness: millboard or other bookbinder's board
For a hardcover book, you will also need:
Decorative papers for the cover and/or endpapers
Strong paper for spine and corners
Mull (binder's reinforcing mesh), fine linen or calico

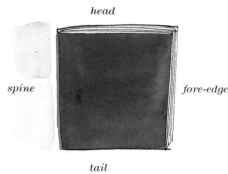

head

spine   fore-edge

tail

A good introduction to basic bookbinding techniques which require the minimum of sewing, is the simple book made of one section only with a soft wrapper-type cover attached by means of turn-ins and flaps.

The first stage is to fold and cut the paper for the book itself. The format of the book will depend on the grain direction of your paper. To see the possibilities for different spread sizes, experiment by folding a spare sheet of paper in half vertically or horizontally according to the grain and then open it out and fold each half in half again and so on. If you now fold the sheet the other way across the grain you will be able to see the final page size.

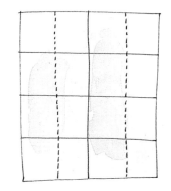

You can make up the section, or block of paper, in two ways. The first method involves folding and is most suitable for larger sheets and for when you are not working to a specific size book. The second method using pre-cut sheets is most appropriate when you know exactly what size and shape you want your book to be, or when you are working with sheets which are too small or thick to fold more than once. This method will also enable you to mix the papers in the section, either for a variety of textures such as tissue alternated with thicker paper, or for colour contrast.

Method 1
Fold the paper in halves, quarters or eighths and so on until you reach the size required, remembering to keep the spine parallel with the grain direction in order to avoid unwanted creases forming at the folds. In this way you can make one complete section from a single sheet of paper (slit at the edges to form the pages) but several folded sheets may be put inside each other to make a fuller section. If the paper is bulky, however, avoid too many insertions – added thickness at the centre sections affects the thickness and projection of the sheets at the fore-edge.

Once you are satisfied with the size and shape of your section, slit the folded edge at the fore-edge (and tail if necessary) and at the top or "head" almost to the centre "gutter" fold. This will enable you to keep the pages together for sewing and trimming, yet give them enough movement to sit comfortably without making creases at the bulky centre fold.

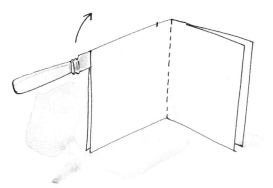

Method 2

With this method the paper is pre-cut to size and the only fold you will need to make will be at the central gutter spine.

Test the possibilities for shape and size on a spare sheet of paper, taking care to fold with the grain direction. Cut the paper to the required size and fold in half to form pages, using a bone folder to help. Don't use excessive pressure or you could stretch and mark the paper, or even crease it; instead, smooth it firmly away from you along its length. If you are using thick paper, you will need to pre-crease the fold; otherwise pre-creasing is not necessary.

Whichever method you have used to assemble your section, it will need to be secured by sewing. At the gutter fold, pre-prick an odd number of evenly-spaced holes. (A small book, about A5 size, will probably need only 3 holes, whereas a large folio size book may need as many as 7 or 9.)

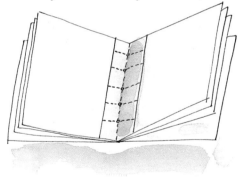

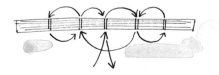

You can measure the distances for the holes with a ruler, but it is easier to make a measuring strip with a narrow piece of scrap paper the length of the section; fold it in half and continue folding to the halfway mark until you have the right number of points.

Now fold in half lengthways; place the 'V' into the inside fold and prick through the measuring strip and the section, holding the strip in place with a clip or peg or a pin placed in the first hole if necessary.

Take a length of thread approximately two and a half times the length of the fold, and thread the needle. Prevent it from slipping off by passing it through the short length of the thread, rather than by making a knot which would enlarge the holes.

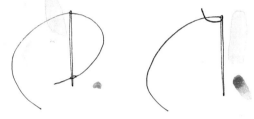

Remove the measuring strip and sew, working firmly from the centre and pulling the thread in the direction of working to prevent tearing the fold.

Start sewing by passing the needle through the centre hole from the outside of the section to the inside and continue as shown in the diagram. After sewing, tie the thread ends in a reef knot over the long centre stitch.

You will now need to trim the head, tail and fore-edge to neaten the edges, ensuring that you retain the right angles which give the book its neat "square" shape. For the fore-edge, measure and lightly mark two points equidistant from the back fold or spine to the fore-edge, then use a set square or carpenter's square to mark points or straight lines for trimming the head and tail at right angles to spine and fore-edge. Using the points as a guide, trim the three edges with a knife held vertically against a straight edge and drawn carefully through one or two leaves at a time, holding the book in place with a weight if necessary.

For single section books you can make a simple wrapper cover which will not need to be sewn but is simply tucked in or interwoven with the first page of the book. Measure a piece of thick, coloured, patterned or laminated paper. It should be the same height as the section, but three times its width.

Fold the paper in half widthways, pre-creasing stiff paper or card with a bone folder. If the section is thick, allow for the spine by marking out its width on the covering paper with two parallel pre-creased lines. Place the spine of the section against the centre fold of the paper, and mark where the fore-edge comes. Fold in the flaps at back and front around the first and last leaves of the book.

For a stronger, more secure cover, allow extra covering paper at the length as well as the width, and make a turn-in at the head and tail to slot together with the fore-edge flap. Cut a small 'V' at head and tail at the spine to allow for the extra thickness of the paper.

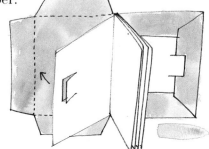

To make some decorative variations you can weave the flyleaf or first leaf of the section through the cover paper: make a template for the design cut to the size of the book and use it to cut first the cover then the flyleaf so that all the widths to be slotted through are neatly aligned.

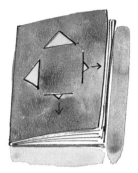

Alternatively, wrap two extra coloured sheets around the outside of the section before sewing; then thread them through the cover to provide the woven pattern with colour contrast. These sheets are known as endpapers since they are extra to the flyleaves – spare or blank sheets – at either end of the book. If you don't want to weave them, use these pages merely as a pleasant transition between the cover and the main body of the book.

You can make books out of single sheets of paper rather than folded sections, using a method based on Japanese book-making. Japanese paper is best suited to these books as it is softer and more flexible than Western types; it can even be used doubled at the fore-edge and stitched at the cut edge.

You can make the covers out of thicker coloured paper or thin paper turned in over the edges of a sheet the same size as the book and glued at the turn-ins only. This is then covered with a paper complementing the book and cover. It would usually be tipped at the edges, leaving the rest of the area more flexible than if the whole cover had been glued or pasted down.

Assemble the block of sheets to be sewn, supported by two pieces of card, and shake the edges into alignment by knocking them down against a flat surface. This side will form the spine. Knock to the head as well and again to the spine.

Hold the block between fingers and thumbs and tap the head downwards on a flat surface. Carefully quarter rotate and tap

down spine. Holding the block carefully, lay it down flat. Put a weight on top to hold it in place while you are marking it out for sewing.

At least ¼in (0.5cm) in from the spine edge, mark a series of evenly spaced dots at any distance apart but not less than ⅜in (1cm). Keep the book steady, either against a right angle or straight edge, with the weight still in place. Make holes at the marked dots using a sharp point or bradawl. Sew temporary holding stitches between the holes to hold the paper together as a block; then trim the edges a few leaves at a time using a sharp point or bradawl, and holding the blade vertically against the rule. Cut two pieces of card for the covers to match the size of the block. Cover them as desired. Mark them, using one sheet as a template, so that the sewing points are aligned and the edges correspond with those of the book.

Sew the book and covers together using coloured silks or embroidery thread if you really want to make an attractive feature of the stitching. The thread should be three times the length of the book plus approximately 12in (30cm) for ease of working. Sew from one end of the book using a running stitch until you reach the other end, then take the thread over the spine and come back through the same hole. Make a stitch now at right angles to the running stitches as shown in the diagram below.

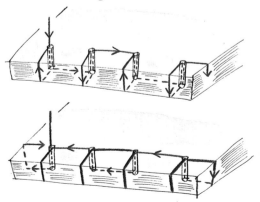

To finish off, remove the needle and take the thread over the head/tail, so that the two loose ends are together. Tie them in a reef knot close to the nearest hole then pull the thread through so that the knot is concealed in the spine. Cut off the ends on the outside close to the hole.

If the cover appears to open stiffly, run a pre-creasing line with a bone folder about ¼in (3−4mm) from the holes.

Albums

You could make a chunky version of this book into an album, by adding extra strips or "guards" between each sheet at the spine, to compensate for the photographs or whatever you are pasting in. Use heavy-weight paper and pre-crease each sheet. Allow 1in (2.5cm) for the spine, plus another ½in (1cm) to cover the amount you will lose in the opening. If you are using a stiffer cover, make sure you have a generous gap between the spine strip and the cover to allow for flexing at the joint (see page 135, where the same method is described for making folders).

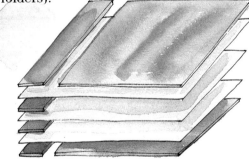

You may need to use a punch or drill holes with a hand drill. You can then use cord to thread through the holes – which should be large enough to take the cord comfortably. This method allows you to insert or remove sheets if you wish.

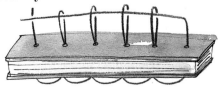

Far left: *Torn sheets in a harmonizing colour, were glued onto the blue cover before it was wrapped around the book. The other two books show some of the interesting geometrical patterns that can be created by weaving the endpapers through the covers.*

Above: *Coloured silks and simple, imaginative stitching are the distinctive features of these "Japanese" books. Use paper you have either bought or decorated yourself to give the covers an individual and professional finish.*

AN INVENTIVE ALTERNATIVE

This is a simple, oriental form of book. Not only does it make an attractive and exciting gift, but it can also be especially useful for recording and storing certain types of information and work, for example, maps, charts, tables – anything which is spread over a number of pages – since the concertina can be opened out, exposing several pages at once, or temporarily juxtaposing two pages from different parts of the book.

You can make a concertina or zig-zag book from one long sheet of paper, but for a book with more than just a few pages, you may have to join several sheets (remembering to join them according to their grain direction). A neat way to do this is to cut and fold the paper as you did for the single-section books, then tip the edges and insert the folds alternately.

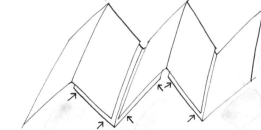

Make sure all the folded sheets are parallel at the fore-edge with the spine, and are all of exactly the same width. Press the sheets together firmly and trim the head and tail at right angles to the folded edges.

To make very simple covers which are glued to the first and last pages of the concertina, cover two thin boards with decorative paper, turning it on all four edges. Insert a sheet of waste paper under the first leaf of the book. Paste up the flyleaf and carefully place the board on. Repeat for the second flyleaf and board, then leave them to dry, protecting the book from damp by using sheets of wax paper or polythene on either side.

Alternatively, you can make a more integrated and sophisticated cover, again from decorated boards, which looks highly professional but is actually surprisingly simple.

The cover paper can be decorative paper you have either bought or made yourself. If it is fairly thin, it can be textured or crinkled before being wrapped around the boards. You can achieve a very interesting finish by embossing the paper (a raised image rather than a pressed one). This is done by damping some strong paper, preferably hand made, and pressing it over a raised pattern stuck onto a piece of board. String coated with PVA and sprayed with silicone to prevent sticking, can give you some unusual effects, reminiscent of early Celtic decorative elements and Nordic scroll patterns.

Remember if you are using paper which has a motif or central decorated area, to position it carefully so that the pattern is properly placed in relation to the cover.

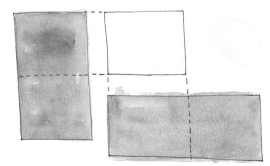

Cut two thin boards to the size of the book and two pieces of cover paper for each board – one plain piece the same width as the board but twice its height (B), and one patterned piece the same height as the board but twice its width (A).

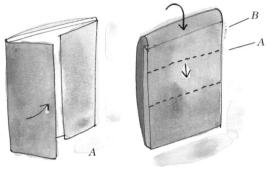

Wrap the pieces, A, around each board, paying attention to the positioning of the pattern if there is one. Join the two boards

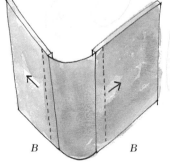

together with a strip of matching paper laid across them to form a spine, pasting the overlaps down onto the A wrappers, which will eentually be covered with the B wrappers, as shown above. (If you are making a thick book, pre-crease the spine.) Pre-crease the second pieces, B. Wrap each one lengthways around one of the boards, tucking the flaps into the slots between the continuous side of the A wrapper and the board itself, as shown in the diagram (top right).

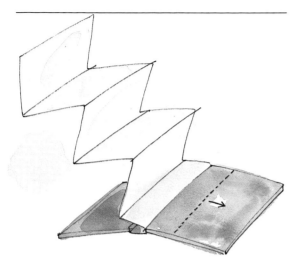

To put the book together, take the concertina insert and slot the end leaves X and Y, into the wrapper between the layers of covering paper.

An attractive spiral pattern made by embossing the paper with carefully arranged string, cleverly echoes the S-shape of the concertina within and adds interest to a plain cover.

PAPERBACK ELEGANCE

For a thicker book or one with more pages than can be made from a single section, two or more sections can be joined together by sewing. The method may appear complicated at first, but with practice, you will soon master the technique.

Method for two-section book
Fold two sections (using either of the methods described on pages 140–1) with three or four folded sheets per section depending on the thickness of the paper and the size of book you want. Any paper can be used but writing paper or cartridge paper, being strong, are most suitable, at least to begin with.

Having assembled the sections, mark points for sewing using the measuring strip method explained on page 141. Measure the thread and secure it as before. Then sew as shown below:

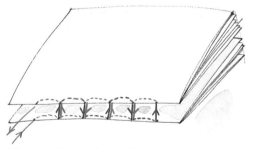

The red shows the path of the first row of stitching; the green shows the return journey of the thread, filling in the missing stitches and reinforcing those linking the sections to each other.

Sew, starting from the outside of the first section and going from the first to the second hole on the inside forming a stitch; to the outside again and up through the parallel hole on the second section, make a stitch then go back to the parallel hole on the first section. Continue to the end of the row, then return, filling in the stitches missed on the first journey.

Tie the two threads with a reef knot on the outside at first and last holes.

You can make a wrapper cover for the two-section book exactly as for the single section book, but in this case, since there are more pages, you will have to make a double pre-creased spine to accommodate the spine width of the section. You could wrap a spare piece of paper around the sections and then use it as a template for the cover paper.

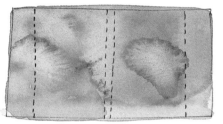

Tuck the inner flaps over the first and last leaves of the book, or add endpapers which match or contrast with the cover paper:

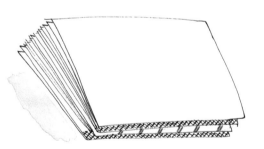

These can be tipped in at the spine edges, gluing the section rather than the endpaper, or you can attach the cover using the method suggested for single-section books on pages 141–2.

Method for multi-section book
The sewing method for this type of book is especially useful for four or more sections. The number of sewing points is again even and will depend on the size of the book. As with the two-section book, each section is stitched to the other and joined on the outside with a link stitch at each sewing point.

Knock up the sections to the spine and head, then mark for sewing points: making the first point ⅜in (10mm) in from the head, and the second ½in (12mm) up from the tail. (The allowance at the tail is greater than at the head since the knocking up will push the unevenness of the paper to the tail, which will then have to be trimmed.)

Measure two, four or six points equidistant between the end holes. Calculate the length of thread by multiplying the distance between two holes by eight, and then adding approximately 12in (30cm) for ease of working. Unlike most sewing methods, a needle is attached to each end of the thread.

Secure the thread as usual, then begin the first section by passing the needles through adjacent holes in pairs from the inside of the first section to the outside.

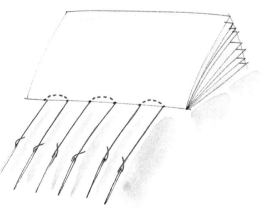

Lay the next section on top, then pass the threads through the corresponding holes of the second section from outside in. Cross the threads on the inside of the section then pass them back through the same holes. Place the third section on, pass the needles through the corresponding holes, cross them over on the inside of the section and back through the holes; and so on until all the sections have been attached.

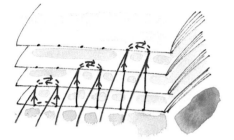

You will now find that the first section sewn is not as secure as the others. To join it, pass the needle behind the linking stitches joining the sections, starting at the top and working your way back to the bottom, or first-sewn section, as shown in the diagram below.

To finish off, pass one needle back through the hole in the first section and bring the needle out at the next hole along so that the two ends of thread are together. These can then be joined in a reef knot.

This book can be covered with a "limp" unglued wrapper-type cover similar to the one used to cover a two-section book; but because it has more sections it would be advisable to add endpapers for extra protection, tipped in at front and back. Alternatively, you could make a hard cover as described in the section on hardcover books, pages 150–2.

Limp cover sewn with the book

This early Western system of bookbinding, dating back as far as the sixteenth century, is still very popular today, especially with conservationists. It is distinctive in its use of high-quality, handmade papers, as in the example on page 149, with a cover of heavy English paper handmade from flax fibres.

You can have as many sections as you wish, but five or more will show up the pattern of the stitching on the spine. Form the sections and trim as usual. You could trim only the head of the book, leaving the fore-edge and tail untrimmed or "rough" cut to reveal the deckle edge of handmade paper, or to give an unusual finish to machine-made or mould-made paper. If you are leaving uneven edges, you can protect the book from damage to some extent by storing it on its side rather than upright. Any edges which do need trimming, however, should be trimmed now since the sewing holes will have to be quite close to the final edges in order to attach the book securely to the cover.

Pre-prick the holes for sewing ⅜in (1cm) away from each edge, with the others equidistant between them.

Measure the covering paper according to the dimensions of the sections and allow for the spine and turn-ins – approximately 2in

(5cm) at head and tail and 2½in (6.5cm) at the fore-edge.

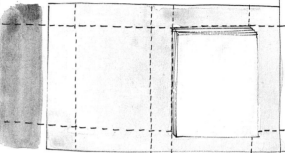

These measurements are intended as a guide only since it's really a matter of personal preference, but you should not make the turn-ins too narrow or they will be difficult to handle.

Compress the sections slightly, under weights if necessary, and then measure the width of the spine. Allow for the natural spring of the paper: if the spine is too compressed the book can assume a wedge shape as air gets trapped between the leaves.

It would be useful at this stage to make a kind of template of the spine, marking on it the sewing points and the distance between sections (which can be considerable if you are using handmade paper or bulky

sections). Transfer these marks to the cover paper, since this will be wrapped around the book during sewing, indicating with parallel lines of pin pricks the width of the spine, and of the individual sections.

At the head and tail prick points for the turn-in flaps. You should allow a small projection called the "square" approximately ³⁄₁₆in (2–3mm) beyond the head and tail of the text block to protect it from dust and damage.

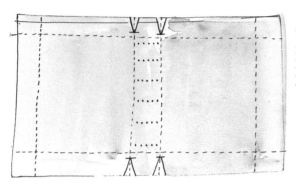

You can adopt the old method of protecting the book with a "yap" edge – a small width bent over at the fore-edge. To do this, add an extra ½in (1cm) to the width of the cover on either side.

Pre-crease the cover at the spine joints to correspond with the width of the book at the spine. Allow an extra ³⁄₁₆in (2mm) to keep the action of the cover separate from the action of the paper.

In fact it will be necessary to pre-crease thick paper at every point where folding occurs.

Cut small "V" shapes at the spine on the turn-in as far as the "square" depth.

Thread a needle with a long piece of linen thread: cord no. 35 which is of medium thickness, is probably the most suitable.

Keep the sections flat and work with the spine at the edge of the work surface, or raise the pieces on several pressing boards to enable you to get at the folds.

Begin sewing inside the first section emerging at point "A" (the second hole along) on the outside of the cover. Sew running stitches along the first section. When you get to the end, lay the next section on top and pass the needle from the outside of the last sewn hole to the hole of the new section immediately above it. Sew along this second section and continue adding further sections in the same way. In this way, the cover is attached at the same time as the sections are being sewn.

When you reach the top, work your way back filling in the stitches that have been missed out, and finishing at the head/tail hole of the first section, next to the starting point A.

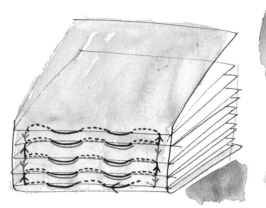

If you run out of thread, attach another length with a weaver's knot to the old one on the inside of a section, rather than at a stitch which links one section to another.

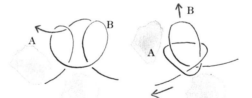

To make a weaver's knot, pass loop B behind A and through to make a slip knot that runs on the long thread. Place on the old thread close to the spine and pull the two lengths of the new thread to form a firm slip knot. The old thread will be drawn through with a firmness that prevents slipping.

Once you have finished the sewing, fold in the fore-edge flaps of the cover, pre-creasing as before, and using the bone folder against a straight edge to form the fold. Leave a square as at head and tail of ⅛–³⁄₁₆in (2–3mm) which extends beyond the block. Trim excess thickness at the head and tail on the turn-in.

There are several ways to tuck the corners into each other. Two methods are suggested below:

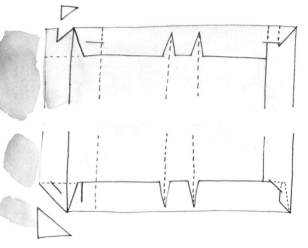

If you have allowed for a yap, tuck or turn in the corners, then pre-crease and fold over the ¼in (5mm) yap allowance.

You can make a limp cover which is laced onto a multi-section book after sewing. The technique is slightly more complicated than those explained above, but is the most widely used by more experienced bookbinders. The method involves sewing the book onto tapes with endbands for extra strength. The tapes are then laced through slots in the cover and tied or buckled at the fore-edge.

You can make single-section hardcover books as described on the following pages. However, multi-section hardcover books should be sewn on tapes for extra strength.

High-quality handmade paper has been used for these elegant books. Remember to do any embossing or decorating before you put the cover on.

SIMPLE HARDCOVERS

For added strength and protection or for a really special gift, you may find that you prefer the more permanent and luxurious feel of a hardcover.

The sewing systems for the sections of these books are the same as those used for limp covered ones, but the hard covers provide a good basis for your decorative papers. You can adapt the covering techniques used for boxes and follow the usual rules for grain direction, different types of adhesive and the effects of pasting paper onto card.

A hardcover book is made in two parts: the sewn book block and the cover, which are then pasted together.

Single-section Books

Prepare a section following the instructions provided on pages 140–1. The endpapers can either be folded round the section before sewing, or glued (to a width of ¼in/6mm) and tipped in along the spine.

Press, and trim the fore-edge so that it is parallel with the spine. Trim the head and tail "square" – at right angles to the spine. Cut a strip of mull, stiffened calico or fine linen just short of the book's length and 2in (5cm) wide and fold it in half along its length. Glue the section 1in (2.5cm) in from the spine on back and front, then stick the band to the spine.

The casing-in method is the same,

whether you have sewn the endpapers or tipped them in, but in the sewn method the stitches at the spine will be apparent.

Cut the boards to the size of the book with the sides at right angles to each other. For the length, allow ⅛in (2mm) extra for the "square", or overlap, beyond the head and tail. For the width, place the board ³⁄₁₆in (4mm) in from the spine (for a flexible joint) and allow an overlap beyond the fore-edge of ³⁄₁₆in (4mm) to enable the board to draw back a little in use, and to provide extra protection at the most vulnerable edge. These proportions apply to standard A4 and A5 books, but whichever size or shape book you are covering, for the sake of balance, the overlap should generally equal the thickness of the board.

Cut the cover paper roughly to the size of a double spread, but allow an extra millimetre or so more than the width of the spine. On the length allow an extra ⅝in (15mm) for each of the turn-ins at head, tail and fore-edge. Trim one long and one short side at right angles to each other.

With dividers and a set square mark two points lightly on the reverse of the cover paper ⅝in (15mm) in from each edge.

Using PVA, glue up the first board and lay it on the paper up to the points marked. Press down, ensuring that the edges are secure enough not to pull away.

Place the book on the board with the fore-edge squares parallel (you may find it easier to pre-mark the position with dividers). The spine will be overhanging the board at the centre by ³⁄₁₆in (4mm).

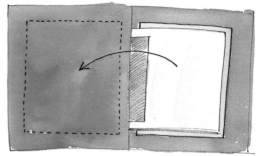

Holding the book steady, mark the paper with a pencil held vertically against the spine. Note the measurement between the board edge and the central pencil mark. Repeat this width on the other side of the pencil mark, and mark the distance. You can work either from left to right or *vice versa*.

Glue up the second board: hold the rule against the top edge of the first board, place the second board up to the rule and against the width mark and press down firmly.

Fold the corners of the paper over onto the board to determine the angle for cutting.

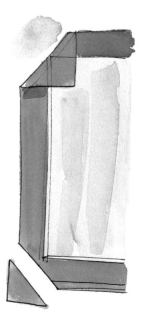

Cut away from the corner at this angle to a measurement equal to the thickness and a half of the board. If the board is ⅛in (2mm) then cut ³⁄₁₆in (3mm) in from the corner. Place the paper and boards on waste paper, glue up the turn-in area, head first and then tail, and use a clean area of waste to turn over the turn-ins onto the board. Press down, with the help of a bone folder, especially at the corners. Next, turn in the fore-edges. These should sit neatly as long as the turn-ins were smoothed well down and flush with the edge of the board.

You are now ready to case in the book. Tuck a sheet of waste paper under the first endpaper leaf to prevent glue from seeping into the rest of the book. Using paste/PVA mixture (which allows time for working and adjusting the paper if necessary), carefully paste up the endpaper, then place the pasted side down in position on the inside of the cover, with the spine up to the centre of allowance as shown in the following diagram.

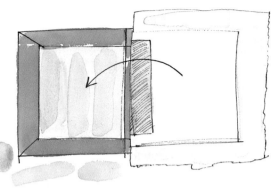

Without pulling the endpaper right back, partially open the book to check that the squares are even at head and tail and parallel at the fore-edge. Smooth gently to push out the air pockets. Close. Paste up the second endpaper, remove the waste paper, hold down with tips of fingers of one hand to prevent curling of pasted paper. With forefinger and thumb holding outside spine to book spine, ease the board over and down to align with its partner.

Gently press, then turn book over to check squares, air pockets and positioning. Slip a piece of water resistant paper at each end between the board and book to prevent damp from the glue penetrating the book. Press overnight. Next day, remove the water resistant paper and gently ease the boards at the hinge towards the book where the join is. Easing at this stage prevents the cover from being strained when the book is in use.

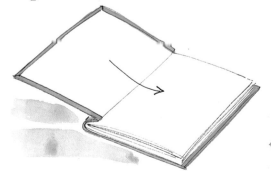

Provided you do not make the book too

thick, you can use this method for multi-section books as well. To strengthen the spine and prevent the sections from distorting the book by sliding over each other, brush a layer of PVA across the sections, pushing it in carefully and pressing along the length for even distribution.

Press between boards under a weight until dry. Trim in the usual way. Apply the mull or calico reinforcement strip as before, and cut the boards for the cover. You will need to add a liner of paper the length and width of the spine for extra support. You will also need to add a stiffener of card the same length as the boards, and as wide as the book's spine plus one board's thickness.

To ascertain the stiffener's position, lay the book on the first board, place the stiffener vertically against the spine and mark its edge on the cover paper. Remove the book, lay the stiffener flat against the mark and mark its width. Repeat the joint width to give the position of the next board.

Glue up the stiffener and place it in the spine allowance marked, then proceed as before. To attach the cover, glue up one endpaper and place the book on the board. Hold the spine of the cover vertically against the spine of the book, pressing down on the edge closest to the book in order to retain the "square" back.

If you find the endpaper has stretched at the fore-edge, mark a new, square fore-edge on the paper using dividers. Slip in a rule and with a very sharp blade, carefully trim off the excess strip at the marks. It is helpful to place a strip of wax paper at the fore-edge on the paste/PVA before putting the ends down; then if you have to trim you will be able to pull the excess away easily.

Half and quarter binding

The principles are the same for half and quarter bindings as for full case binding, although the pieces used are smaller – a thin panel at the spine for quarter binding, with an additional panel or corner pieces at the fore-edge for half binding.

Cut the boards to the required size, allowing for the spine width and squares as usual. Make up the spine covering strip – the width is really a matter of personal preference, but for a well-balanced appearance allow about a quarter of the overall width of the board to show. Double this width and add twice the joint allowance plus the width of the spine stiffener. The length of the spine strip will be equal to the length of one board plus two turn-in widths.

The perpendicular measurement of the corners will be equal to the width of the spine strip which is visible on the cover.

Glue the boards onto the chosen width of spine covering strip (as described on page 150). Turn in at head and tail. Cut out corner pieces and side panels of decorative paper. Paste up the side panels using paste/PVA. Gently ease them into position, butting them up to the spine strip. Slide on the corners, gluing the board rather than the pieces, to

butt to the side panels. Alternatively, you could paste down the spine corners first, then apply the side panels, overlapping them as you put them in place. Turn in head, tail and fore-edge. Press. Then case in the book as already described.

You can vary these techniques as you did for the single-section books to produce full, half and quarter cased books. The design variations are as numerous as your imagination can make them – many of the pleating, texturing, crinkling and decorative techniques can be used on the side panels of half and quarter binding as well as on the full-bound books to produce an endless variety of exciting, imaginative and individual designs.

These three half-bound books with their blue and white theme share a muted, traditional feel, yet convey quite different impressions. The intricate woven cover on the left requires some patience and skill to create, and you should perhaps experiment on a smaller area to begin with. Vary the effect by using different colours as well as textures for contrast. The paste and colour method (pages 66–8) has been used to make the three-dimensional looking, shell-like pattern of the central book, and the tie makes a neat finishing touch.

A more startling effect could be achieved with bolder use of contrasting colours. You can reproduce the feel of the classic ledger book of the past with corner pieces and a marbled central panel, as in the book, right. For a more casual finish, follow the method for simple marbling given on page 84.

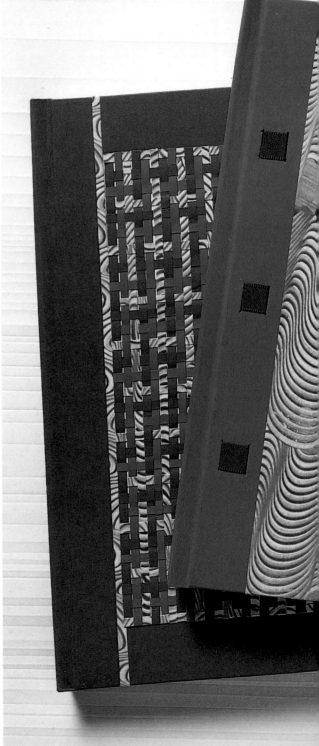

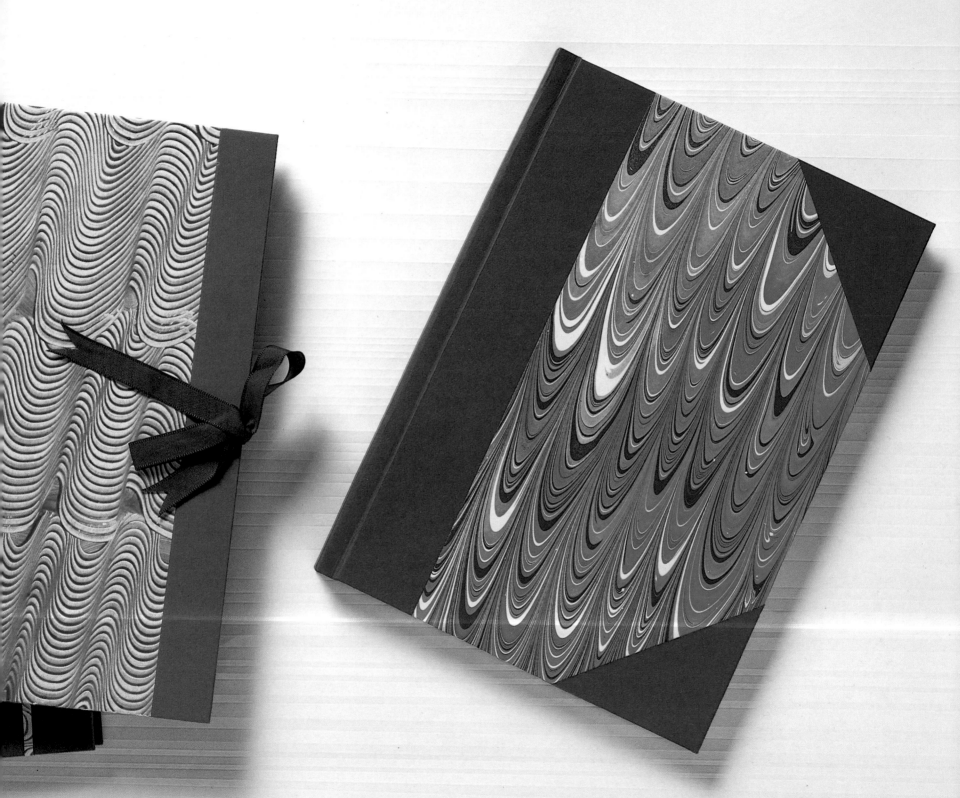

THE BEAUTY OF BENDING THE RULES

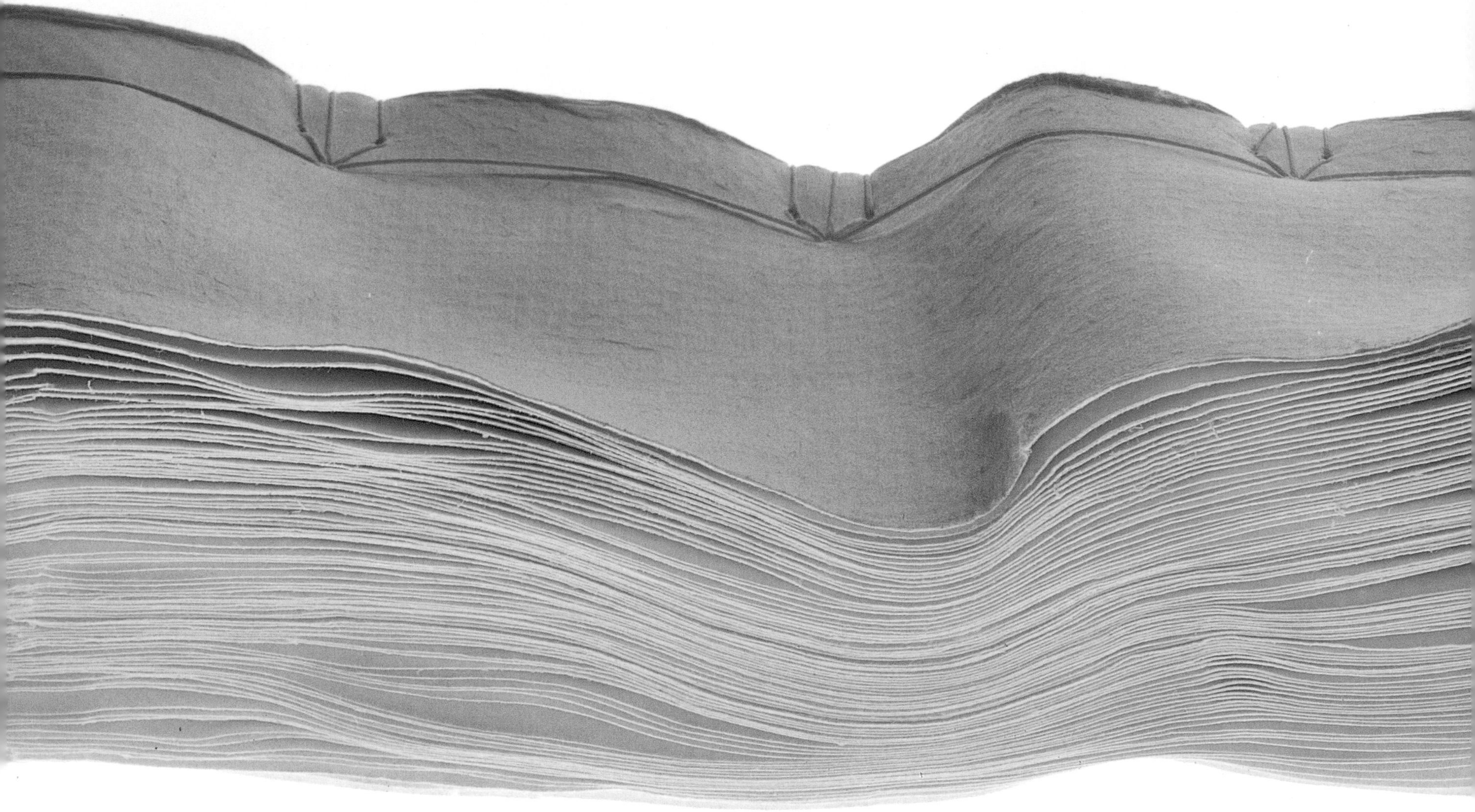

This simple book structure sewn in the Japanese manner has been photographed from two directions — looking onto the fore-edge (on these pages) and onto the spine (overleaf). Both views show the complexities of the book's organic undulating shape, like the gills of a mushroom. The book was designed as an abstract form — it is not intended to be used as a notebook. To achieve the desired effect, sheets of machine-made paper were sewn together against the grain using linen thread. The completed object was then soaked overnight in water. The paper swelled but was con-strained by the taut thread, which caused it to buckle attract-ively. The undulations remained in place after the paper had dried out.

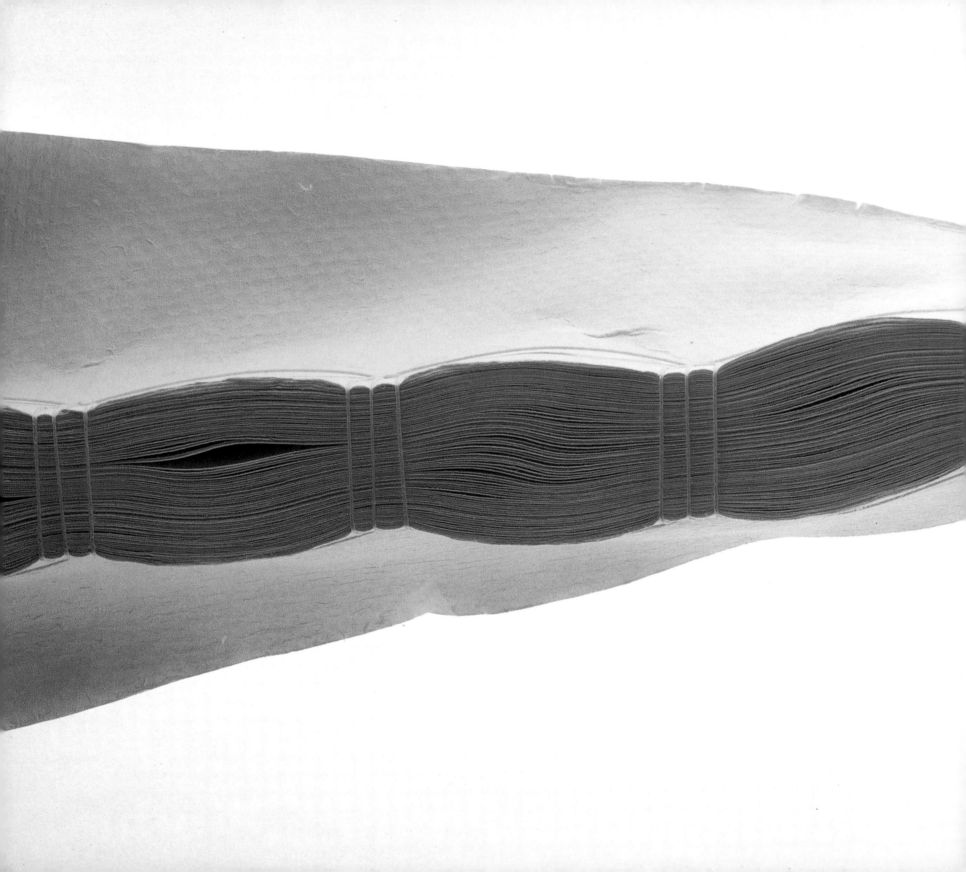

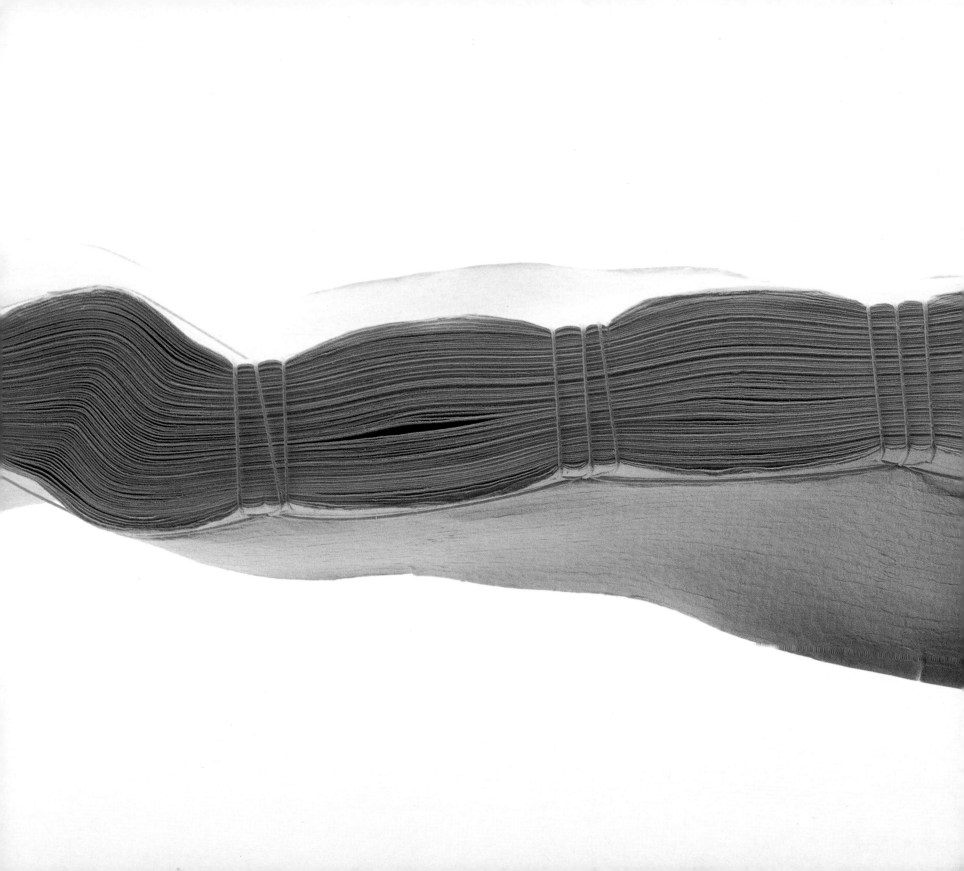